Media, Place and Mobility

Key Concerns in Media Studies

Series editor: Andrew Crisell

Within the context of today's global, digital environment, *Key Concerns in Media Studies* addresses themes and concepts that are integral to the study of media. Concisely written by leading academics, the books consider the historical development of these themes and the theories that underpin them, and assess their overall significance, using up-to-date examples and case studies throughout. By giving a clear overview of each topic, the series provides an ideal starting point for all students of modern media.

Published

Forthcoming

Media, Place and Mobility

Shaun Moores

Professor of Media and Communications, University of Sunderland

First published 2012 by
PALGRAVE MACMILLAN

Palgrave Macmillan in the UK is an imprint of Macmillan Publishers Limited, registered in England, company number 785998, of Houndmills, Basingstoke, Hampshire RG21 6XS.

Palgrave Macmillan in the US is a division of St Martin's Press LLC, 175 Fifth Avenue, New York, NY 10010.

Palgrave Macmillan is the global academic imprint of the above companies and has companies and representatives throughout the world.

Palgrave® and Macmillan® are registered trademarks in the United States, the United Kingdom, Europe and other countries

ISBN-13: 978–0–230–24463–4

This book is printed on paper suitable for recycling and made from fully managed and sustained forest sources. Logging, pulping and manufacturing processes are expected to conform to the environmental regulations of the country of origin.

A catalogue record for this book is available from the British Library.

A catalog record for this book is available from the Library of Congress.

10   9   8   7   6   5   4   3   2   1
21 20 19 18 17 16 15 14 13 12

Printed and bound in Great Britain by
CPI Antony Rowe, Chippenham and Eastbourne

Electronic media affect us ... by changing the 'situational geography' of social life.

(Meyrowitz, 1985, p. 6)

When space feels thoroughly familiar to us, it has become place.

(Tuan, 1977, p. 73)

If we take mobility to be a defining characteristic of the contemporary world, we must ... ask how, in a world of flux, forms of ... dwelling are sustained and reinvented.

(Morley, 2000, pp. 12–13)

Contents

Preface and Acknowledgements

I want to start by reflecting briefly on an aspect of my personal experience, because it provides me with an initial way into the key concerns of this book. A few years ago, I left Britain for a while and spent some time living and working in Australia, having taken up a position at a university there. During the early months in that new country, there were many environmental differences that I very much appreciated, not least of which was the warmth of late summer and autumn in Melbourne, after leaving the cold of midwinter in the north of England. However, to my surprise, there were also a number of quite ordinary things that I missed from my life in the UK (things that I had not anticipated missing). For instance, although my new journey into work was exhilarating, cycling across parkland with the city's skyscrapers rising up before me as I rode, I found myself recalling the old drive to and from my university, and especially the voices on my preferred British radio station, which had routinely accompanied me on those car journeys. From Australia, I could access that station live via the internet, enabling me to hear its familiar sounds, and yet I had an increasingly detached experience of listening, perhaps partly as a result of the mismatch between the UK time-checks, weather or traffic reports and my everyday physical surroundings in Melbourne. In the same period, I found that my first experiences of watching Australian television, while sitting on somebody else's sofa in a rented house, were predominantly ones of strangeness. Although a few of the programmes were known to me already, usually because they were American dramas that had also been screened in Britain, the various television personalities, channels and schedules were unfamiliar. Still, after a year or so in Melbourne, my fingers were moving effortlessly around the buttons on the remote-control device, and I no longer had to search constantly through the listings in order to discover what was on. In addition, as my partner, my young daughter and I were meeting new people and gradually finding our feet in Australia, we valued email, webcam and telephone contact with absent family members and friends in the UK. On most mornings, for example, our home computer was turned on to read messages from across the globe, which had been deposited for us in the inbox overnight. There was an occasional exchange of cards and gifts via the international postal system, too, and the very occasional visit in person from a relative or friend who had flown over.

So how might these reflections relate to what follows in the pages ahead? Let me now try to indicate at least some of the issues that I see arising from them. To begin with, it is worth noting that my experiences involved using a range of electronic media (radio, television, telephone and computer) and engaging in various forms of technologically mediated communication. It is also worth noting that the experiences I have described were not only to do with practices of media use. I referred there, in addition, to feelings about the weather and a piece of household furniture, as well as to cycling, driving and the movements of objects or people by air. Based on the assumption that I am not alone in experiencing a range of media technologies within the wider circumstances of everyday living, my general approach in this book is one which deals with a variety of contemporary communications (not just those that are associated with the traditional mass media), and one which attempts to understand everyday media uses by considering them alongside many other social practices today, rather than as isolated activities.

More specifically, though, my reflections are related to issues of place and mobility. There is the obvious point here that transnational migration involves a shift in physical location, moving from one country to another, but I will argue in this book that place is more than location. Of course, people's physical locations are important. In the case of my immediate family, the decision to move to Australia and, indeed, our subsequent decision to return to Britain, were both based on lengthy and difficult considerations of the relative merits of different locations from our particular perspective. It is possible, too, to see how media offer locations or spaces of a sort to occupy, such as television channels and email inboxes, as media users simultaneously occupy a physical environment. However, my personal story points to something more about place, which is its experiential dimension. Places are formed through repetitive, habitual practices that give rise to emotional or affective attachments to environments. For example, the emotional connection that I feel with my favourite radio station was developed over time through routine acts of listening while driving, as well as listening in the house. This sound environment had become a taken-for-granted feature of my everyday experience, to the extent that I only came to realise its significance for me when it was no longer readily available and was therefore missed. In other words, it was migration's disruption of routine that enabled me to see that I am at home in this media space, and, interestingly, when I did eventually return to the UK, I similarly felt the absence of the Australian media with which I had become familiar. I will be arguing, in addition, that various mobilities help to constitute senses of place at different geographical scales. The kinds of mobility that I referred to in my account include practices of cycling or driving to work, of manipulating a remote-control device and of travelling imaginatively and virtually across vast distances via electronic media. All of these movements served to facilitate my place-making, and the story that I have told suggests how technologically mediated communication contributes, in significant ways, to what has been called the openness of places in contemporary society.

In the chapters to follow, I explore such issues in a wide-ranging discussion of academic literature. For the most part, then, my book offers a critical synthesis of relevant theoretical perspectives on media, place and mobility. However, I should make it clear that I do not value theory simply for its own sake. In my view, the details of theoretical debate are certainly important, and I am committed to explaining these in an accessible manner, but I am also committed to finding theories that can help to explain the details of everyday living.

Although it only took me a year or so to write the book, my thoughts on media, place and mobility have been developing over a much longer period (for instance, see Moores, 2004, 2006, 2007, 2008; Moores and Metykova, 2009, 2010), and the arguments that are presented in the pages ahead were initially rehearsed in something close to their current form in my inaugural professorial lecture at the University of Sunderland. I am grateful to Andrew Crisell, my good colleague and series editor, who attended that lecture and later invited me to contribute to his new book series on key concerns in media studies. Andy's series provides an ideal context for this book, because I am writing for students who are on undergraduate and taught postgraduate programmes in media studies, or who are taking media-related modules elsewhere in the social sciences and humanities. At the same time, I hope that the book will be of considerable interest to fellow academics in my field, because I am proposing a revision of the type of media studies that is usually taught in universities.

I am grateful, too, to Monika Metykova, formerly a postdoctoral fellow at the University of Sunderland's Centre for Research in Media and Cultural Studies, who was my highly able co-researcher on the project that is discussed at the close of the third chapter. More generally, I would like to acknowledge the institutional support of the Centre for Research in Media and Cultural Studies, where I am fortunate to have many good colleagues. Thanks in particular to Lianne Hopper for her patience in dealing with my numerous printing requests, and to John Storey and Eve Forrest, who took the time to read parts of the book in draft form before talking through some of the ideas with me. In Eve's case, this was while I supervised her postgraduate research on the routine practices of photographers in urban and online environments.

When my thoughts on media, place and mobility were starting to come together, I was based in the Faculty of Arts at the University of Melbourne. Among my fond memories of this time are those that I have of reading phenomenological geography in a well-stocked university library, as well as in some of Melbourne's well-stocked cafes! I also have fond memories of my subsequent, shorter stay at the University of Bremen in Germany, where I was a visiting professor in the Faculty of Cultural Studies, and I am grateful to Andreas Hepp for his hospitality and for lively discussions of theory. More recently, I accepted invitations to deliver lectures at Uppsala University and Karlstad University in Sweden, where I had helpful conversations with André Jansson, a communications geographer. Within the UK, I am grateful to the organisers of two conferences for invitations to speak about aspects of my developing work, leading to plenary papers at the Media, Communication and Cultural Studies Association Conference at the University of Bradford and the Transforming Audiences Conference at the University of Westminster.

Next, I am happy to acknowledge the influence that David Morley's work has had on my own thinking, without in any way suggesting that he would agree with all of my arguments. Dave's *Home Territories: Media, Mobility and Identity* (2000) is a pioneering study of media, place and mobility, and I was pleased to accept an invitation a while back to talk about my ideas with his media audiences/geographies students at Goldsmiths College, University of London. I also want to acknowledge the important influence of Paddy Scannell's work. Paddy supervised the undergraduate dissertation that I wrote at the Polytechnic of Central London in the mid-1980s (a dissertation on early radio's incorporation into everyday living, which fired my enthusiasm for investigating quotidian cultures). It is a long time since we last met face to face (he has been working in the US), but his turn to phenomenology has helped, from a distance, to shift my own research interests in broadly the same direction. A further influence has been the work of the late Roger Silverstone. Roger's initial academic training was in the discipline of geography, and, in *Television and Everyday Life* (1994), he refers to the phenomenological geographers in a chapter on television and home. Indeed, he reminded me of their relevance when I spoke several years ago at the London School of Economics and Political Science. Still, it was only after moving to the other side of the world that I followed up on this reminder, coming to see the relevance for myself.

Finally, I am deeply grateful to Karen Atkinson for her loving support over the past fifteen years, to our daughters, Eve Atkinson and Ruby Atkinson (who was born towards the end of our stay in Australia), for their cheerful good company, and to my parents, Joe Moores and Brenda Moores, who have been a lifelong source of encouragement.

SM

1 The Situational Geography of Social Life

The title of my first chapter is a phrase drawn from Joshua Meyrowitz's book, *No Sense of Place: The Impact of Electronic Media on Social Behavior* (1985), in which he presents an analysis of the social significance of electronic media that still has relevance for media studies today, more than a quarter of a century after it was published. In the opening sections of the chapter, I will set out my sympathetic critique of Meyrowitz's book. On the one hand, my discussion highlights the continuing importance of his arguments about a transformation in 'the "situational geography" of social life' (ibid., p. 6), but, on the other hand, I take issue with his contention (clearly indicated by the title of his book) that contemporary existence is increasingly 'placeless'. This critique will provide a foundation on which I can then build in the rest of my book, beginning in this chapter with a differently inflected account of electronic media and 'situational geography', suggested by Paddy Scannell's notes on broadcasting and the 'doubling of place' (Scannell, 1996, p. 172). Several specific examples of 'doubling' are discussed towards the end of the chapter, with reference not only to radio and television but also to mobile-phone and internet use in everyday living.

Weaving Strands of Theory

For me, the most remarkable feature of Meyrowitz's book is his theoretical synthesis of 'two seemingly incompatible perspectives' (Meyrowitz, 1985, p. 7). In his introduction to *No Sense of Place*, he explains how this synthesis developed out of some of the reading that he did as an undergraduate student in the US during the late 1960s, when he first engaged with the writings of two academic authors who were working in quite separate areas. One of these authors was Marshall McLuhan (see especially McLuhan, 1994 [1964]; McLuhan and Zingrone, 1997; also Meyrowitz, 2003), who is regarded by Meyrowitz (1985, p. 16) as a pioneer of 'medium theory' (see also Innis, 1951; Meyrowitz, 1994). The other was

Erving Goffman (see especially Goffman, 1990 [1959]; Lemert and Branaman, 1997; also Meyrowitz, 1979), who is associated by Meyrowitz (1985, p. 28) with a sociological tradition of 'situationism'. Both of these authors offered insights that fascinated him, yet he also realised that each of their approaches had its shortcomings. Through his postgraduate research in the 1970s, he came to the view that McLuhan and Goffman, and, more generally, the analytical perspectives of the 'medium theorists' and the 'situationists' (not to be confused with the avant-garde artistic and political activists who were known by this name), 'have complementary strengths and weaknesses' (ibid., 1985, p. 4). Indeed, Meyrowitz (ibid.) states that his book is the result of 'more than a decade of interest in weaving these two strands of theory into one whole cloth'.

In the writings of McLuhan and others working in medium theory, Meyrowitz finds an analysis of media that has a distinctive emphasis on the medium of communication itself. Whereas much mainstream 'media theory' has focused on 'message content' (ibid., p. 20) and its assumed social consequences, medium theorists focus instead on the consequences that media themselves, 'apart from the content they convey' (ibid., p. 16), can have for the organisation of social life. One of the most memorable phrases to emerge from McLuhan's book, *Understanding Media: The Extensions of Man* (1994 [1964], p. 7), is his declaration that 'the medium is the message'. What is crucial for McLuhan (ibid., p. 9), then, is the capacity of any new medium or type of media to alter 'the scale and form of human association and action'. He argues that media of communication act as 'extensions' of the body and senses, transforming the temporal and spatial arrangements of social life. For example, in the case of television and other electronic media, the advent of 'live' communications across potentially vast physical distances has introduced a new kind of simultaneity and interdependence into social life. Meyrowitz welcomes this concern with media and social change, and with issues of time and space (as do I, although it is important not to draw too stark a distinction between 'medium' and 'content', and there is a problem with the 'technological determinism' of medium theory, see Williams, 1990 [1974]). The main limitation identified by Meyrowitz (1985, p. 23) is McLuhan's failure to pursue this interest in media, change and time-space relations by addressing new modes of 'everyday social interaction'.

Meanwhile, in the writings of Goffman and others working in the situationist tradition, Meyrowitz finds a valuable concern with the dynamics of everyday social interaction, and with the social situations that furnish contexts for this interaction. In Goffman's first and probably still his best-known book, *The Presentation of Self in Everyday Life* (1990 [1959]), he 'describes social life using the metaphor of drama' (Meyrowitz, 1985, p. 28), conceptualising interactions and situations in terms of 'performances', 'actors', 'settings' and so forth. Goffman's purpose in employing the vocabulary of the theatre is not simply to claim that 'all the world's a stage', but rather to develop a way of understanding the organisation of 'social encounters ... that come into being whenever persons enter one another's immediate physical presence' (Goffman, 1990 [1959], p. 246). Meyrowitz welcomes that focus on the organisation of 'social encounters' in Goffman's sociology. However, he also identifies a significant limitation, and a clue to this shortcoming is supplied by the reference that Goffman makes to 'immediate physical presence'. In situationism, there has been an overwhelming concern with the study of physically co-present, face-to-face interactions, and a tendency to assume a necessary connection between social situations and physical locations or environments. There has, in addition, been a corresponding tendency to 'ignore interactions ... through media' (Meyrowitz, 1985, p. 33; see also ibid., p. 345, which notes that an exception is Goffman, 1981, although, even there, no serious consideration is given to issues of media and social change).

Clearly, then, McLuhan and Goffman were working on quite different topics. One was studying the consequences of media technologies for changing modes of social organisation, but with little interest in the dynamics of interaction. The other was focusing on interpersonal encounters, but with little regard for the significance of new forms of technologically mediated communication at a distance. It is therefore not too difficult to see how medium theory and situationist sociology might have appeared to Meyrowitz, at the start of his theoretical journey, as 'incompatible perspectives'. Nevertheless, he gradually discovered an inventive way of 'weaving' together these 'strands of theory', linking the analysis of media with the analysis of situated interaction, so that the strengths of each tradition could be combined and their respective weaknesses overcome. Central to the resulting theoretical synthesis or 'whole cloth' is his model of 'situations as information-systems' (Meyrowitz, 1985, p. 35).

Situations as Information-systems

Meyrowitz (1994, p. 58) has described the integrative model that he developed as an instance of 'second-generation medium theory', as distinct from the first generation of which McLuhan's work was a part. In the same way, his model might simultaneously be thought of as an instance of 'second-' or even 'third-generation' situationism (extending the work of Goffman and others in what has also been called 'micro social theory', see Roberts, 2006). Indeed, in order to get a hold on this model of situations as information-systems, it is necessary to revisit Meyrowitz's engagement with situationism, and particularly his insistence that there is no necessary connection between social situations and physical locations. Seeking to dismantle the connection, which the situationists have traditionally taken for granted, Meyrowitz (1985, p. 37) argues that, in the study of situations, it is best to begin with a 'more inclusive notion of "patterns of access to information"' (when he writes of 'access to information' here, he is thinking principally about access to 'social performances' rather than to 'information' as it is more commonly understood, as a set of 'facts' or 'objective statements'). Of course, this 'inclusive notion' does not rule out investigations of face-to-face interpersonal encounters, in which the 'social actors' can access each other's performances in a shared physical location or environment. Crucially, though, it serves to extend the study of situations, allowing also for the investigation of technologically 'mediated encounters' (ibid.), in which there is access to the performances of others who are physically absent. What Meyrowitz's work promises to challenge, then, is a 'distinction often made between studies of face-to-face interaction and studies of mediated communications', and his model of situations as information-systems therefore makes it possible to see 'physical settings and "media settings"' (ibid., pp. 37–8; while I find his terms useful, note that 'media settings' still have a certain physicality or materiality) as overlapping social environments.

Recalling the title of this chapter, it is important to stress that Meyrowitz's theoretical model is designed to deal precisely with a transformation in the situational geography of social life:

> Now ... information is able to flow through walls and rush across great distances ... the social spheres defined by walls ... are ... only one type of interactional environment. ... The theory developed here extends ... to the analysis of social environments created by media of communication ... describes how electronic media affect social behavior – not through the power of their messages but by reorganizing the social settings in which people interact.
>
> (ibid., pp. viii–ix)

For the purposes of my book, this is a particularly helpful quote because, as well as making his fundamental point that electronic media are 'reorganizing the social settings in which people interact', Meyrowitz raises closely related matters to which I will be returning in later chapters. One of these has to do with boundaries and their potential permeability in contemporary society. Another is the matter of technologically mediated 'mobility', which Meyrowitz hints at with his statement that 'information is able to ... rush across great distances'. In this statement, the emphasis is evidently on the electronic movements of social information, but, elsewhere in his book, he gives the point an added twist by suggesting that such information 'flows' can afford experiences of 'travel'. For instance, Meyrowitz (ibid., p. 118) remarks that: 'Through electronic media ... social performers now "go" where they would not or could not.' He adds that people can now feel they are '"present" at distant events' (ibid.) through electronic media use. For the remainder of the current chapter, though, my discussion is focused on what he terms the 'environments created by media of communication' (actually, they are realised in practices of media use), and on the relations between those media settings or 'media environments' (ibid, p. 7) and physical settings of social interaction.

One of Meyrowitz's illustrations of an 'interactional environment' that is formed through media use is the social situation of a telephone conversation:

> We all know from everyday experience that electronic media override the boundaries ... of situations supported by physical settings. When two friends speak on the telephone, for example, the situation they are 'in' is only marginally related to their respective physical locations. Indeed, the telephone tends to bring two people closer to each other, in some respects, than they are to other people in their physical environments. This explains the almost jealous response on the part of some people who are in the same room with someone speaking on the phone. They often ask 'Who is it?' 'What's she saying?' 'What's so funny?'
>
> (ibid., p. 38)

This passage offers an initial example of what is meant by interacting with others in media settings or environments. In the course of everyday living, it would probably be unusual for people speaking on the phone explicitly to think of themselves as being 'in' a media setting (even though the notion of 'immersion' in an environment is quite common nowadays among internet users who are interacting online). Nevertheless, Meyrowitz argues convincingly that, at least for the 'two friends' in his example, there is the 'closeness' of a shared social situation despite their physical separation. Indeed, it may well be that among electronic media the handheld phone is most capable of functioning as an 'intimate' medium of communication, given the technologically mediated proximity of voice to ear in spoken encounters at a distance. As Ian Hutchby (2001, p. 31) puts it, 'intimacy ... is afforded by the telephone' (more generally, see Hutchby's book for an instance of contemporary micro-social theory that does not ignore interactions 'through media'). Still, while Meyrowitz's illustration of a media environment serves a useful purpose here, there is something about his account of the two friends' phone conversation that troubles me. I feel that he could make more of their dual locations, and of the overlaps between a media environment and the physical environments at either end of the line, rather than regarding them as 'only marginally related'. Telephone use, and electronic media use more broadly, is best seen as 'pluralising' social settings, as opposed to removing people from one type of situation, which becomes marginal, and putting them in another. This is a critical point that I will be expanding on in due course.

Para-social Interaction

Meyrowitz (1985, pp. 119–21) goes on to discuss further cases of 'intimacy at a distance' with reference to the work of Donald Horton and Richard Wohl (1956). Interestingly, back in the mid-1950s, Horton and Wohl had already written about the organisation of certain electronically mediated encounters, in a period when television was still establishing itself as an everyday medium, and when McLuhan and Goffman were still in the early stages of their academic careers. For this reason, while I have described Meyrowitz's linking of media analysis with the analysis of situated interaction as the most remarkable feature of his book (a judgement that I stand by), it should be acknowledged that Horton and Wohl had gone at least some of the way down this road many years before. It might be said, then, that they helped to prepare the ground for Meyrowitz's subsequent theoretical synthesis and for his model of situations as information-systems (see also a number of the contributions to Gumpert and Cathcart, 1979, in which Horton and Wohl's article was reprinted).

Horton and Wohl (1956) are particularly interested in what they name the 'para-social interaction' between television hosts or presenters of various sorts and physically absent viewers (see also Thompson, 1995, p. 84, for the derived concept of 'mediated quasi-interaction'; and Jensen, 1999, p. 182, who prefers the term 'social para-interaction'). They note that the performances of television 'personalities' often include looking straight to camera and speaking to viewers as if they were talking sociably with acquaintances or even friends:

> One of the striking characteristics of the new mass media ... is that they give the illusion of face-to-face relationship with the performer. The conditions of response to the performer are analogous to those in a primary group. ... In television, especially, the image which is presented makes available nuances of appearance and gesture to which ordinary social perception is attentive and to which interaction is cued. Sometimes the 'actor' ... uses the mode of direct address, talks as if conversing personally and privately. ... The audience, for its part ... is, as it were, subtly insinuated into the program's action and ... observes and participates in the show by turns. ... This simulacrum of conversational give and take may be called para-social interaction.
>
> (Horton and Wohl, 1956, p. 215)

As Meyrowitz (1985, p. 121) comments, this is 'a new form of interaction' when considered in broad historical terms, and yet, as Horton and Wohl indicate here, it clearly resembles certain features of face-to-face interaction in 'a primary group' (that is, in physically co-present interpersonal encounters). Although performers and viewers are physically separated, there can be a 'simulacrum of conversational give and take'. Of course, unlike a physically co-present, 'face-to-face relationship', the 'para-social relationship' (Horton and Wohl, 1956, p. 215) is a 'non-reciprocal' one, since it 'does not involve the kind of reciprocity and mutuality characteristic of face-to-face interaction' (Thompson, 1995, p. 219; see also Morgan, 2009, pp. 96–7). However, viewers may develop, over time, a sense of 'acquaintanceship', or possibly of 'friendship' and 'intimacy', with television personalities and with other public figures or 'celebrities' who make frequent media appearances. According to Meyrowitz (1985, p. 120), the para-social relationship can become knotted into 'daily ... interactions with friends, family, and associates' in physical settings, such as when, for instance, people 'discuss the antics of their para-social friends'.

A valid objection to these claims about para-social interaction that are made by Horton and Wohl, and echoed by Meyrowitz, would be that they are not backed up with any evidence generated by concrete empirical research. Horton and Wohl state confidently that viewers are 'subtly insinuated into the program's action', but, while they provide a valuable analysis of on-screen performance styles, no 'audience research' findings are actually presented (although see the findings reported by Gauntlett and Hill, 1999, pp. 115–16; and especially by Wood, 2007, 2009). In the case of Meyrowitz's book, there are at least some persuasive reflections, which relate partly to his personal experience of intimacy at a distance, on 'why it is that when a "media friend" such as Elvis Presley, John Kennedy, or John Lennon dies or is killed, millions of people may experience a sense of loss' (Meyrowitz, 1985, p. 120). For example, Meyrowitz (ibid., p. 120) notes that 'the death of John Lennon ... was strangely painful to me and my university colleagues', precisely because they felt they 'had "known" him and grown up "with" him'. More recent examples of this kind of 'grief' are the public responses to the murder of BBC newsreader, Jill Dando, and, on a much larger scale, to the unexpected death of Princess Diana, which I will be discussing later in this chapter with reference to research findings that are reported by Robert Turnock (2000).

A Placeless Culture

Thus far, what I have called my 'sympathetic critique' of *No Sense of Place* has been more sympathetic to Meyrowitz's book than critical of it. I find his weaving of different theoretical strands and the resulting, integrative model to be of continuing importance for media studies, and, more generally, for the investigation of contemporary living. In particular, I welcome the connection that he makes there between social interactions and experiences in both physical and media environments, because it helps to indicate the ways in which media use can '"double" reality' (Scannell, 1996, p. 173). However, there are other aspects of Meyrowitz's book that I find less convincing, and these relate mainly to his assertions about place and 'placelessness'. Up to this point in my discussion of his work, I have deliberately avoided any direct references to place, but I want to focus my critical attention now on Meyrowitz's no-sense-of-place thesis, looking in detail over the coming pages at his argument about electronic media and the emergence of 'a "placeless" culture' (Meyrowitz, 1985, p. 8).

In *No Sense of Place*, the term 'place' is used to refer to 'both social position and physical location' (ibid., p. 308). When defining place as 'social position', Meyrowitz (ibid.) is thinking about the 'social roles' that people play, and about related issues of social identity and hierarchy (what he calls issues of 'social "place"'). When defining place as 'physical location', he is thinking about those interactional environments of immediate physical presence that have been of interest to situationist sociology (issues of 'physical place'). Pulling together these two definitions of the term, Meyrowitz (ibid.) states, with regard to his own national context, that:

> Evolution in media ... has changed the ... social order by restructuring the relationship between physical place and social place ... electronic media, especially television, have had a tremendous impact on Americans' sense of place. ... Many ... no longer seem to 'know their place' because the traditional interlocking components of 'place' have been split apart by electronic media. Wherever one is now – at home, at work, or in a car – one may be in touch and tuned-in. The greatest impact has been on social groups that were once defined in terms of their physical isolation in specific locations – kitchens, playgrounds, prisons ... and so forth. But the changing relationship between physical and social place has affected almost every social role. Our world ... for the first time in modern history ... is relatively placeless.

This is a lengthy quote, and it requires some unpacking in order to get at what Meyrowitz is arguing here about place and placelessness. His fundamental point is that social positions change when electronic media 'override the boundaries' of physical locations. People have traditionally come to 'know their place', he argues, by playing particular social roles in particular interactional environments that are 'defined by walls'. These are 'the traditional interlocking components of place'. When 'patterns of access to information' are altered and new interactional environments are formed, so, from Meyrowitz's perspective, the 'social order' is transformed. He therefore sees identities and hierarchies shifting in what he labels the 'electronic society' (ibid., p. 339).

Two of Meyrowitz's main examples of change are indicated by his mentioning of 'kitchens' and 'playgrounds' (I will turn shortly to 'prisons', the third of the 'specific locations' that he mentions in the quote). Meyrowitz (ibid., p. 224) claims, then, that the arrival of television and other electronic media in the household 'liberates women' from their previous 'informational confines'. Electronic media, he continues, 'weaken the notion of men's spheres and women's spheres' and tend to 'foster a "situational androgyny"' (ibid., pp. 224–5). Similarly, he (ibid., p. 226) proposes that there is a 'blurring of childhood and adulthood' in contemporary society. He observes that television 'now escorts children across the globe even before they have permission to cross the street' (ibid., p. 238; and note that this is another hint at the importance of technologically mediated mobility or travel). As a consequence, according to Meyrowitz (ibid., p. 163), the social identities of children, and relations between children and adults, have shifted:

> Once, teachers and parents had nearly absolute control over the general social information available to the young child. This gave the process of socialization many aspects of hierarchy. Now these authorities are often ... in the position of explaining or responding to social information available directly to children through television.

A further main example offered by Meyrowitz (ibid., p. 168) is the changing relationship between American political leaders and 'the people': 'Through television, "the people" now have more access to the personal expressive behaviors of leaders than leaders have to the personal behaviors of the people.' As John Thompson (1995, pp. 140–1) writes, this 'mediated visibility' is a 'double-edged sword' for political leaders, bringing 'new opportunities' to reach viewers and potential voters, but bringing 'new risks' as well, and a 'new and distinctive kind of fragility' (see also Thompson, 2000, for an analysis of 'political scandal', in which he discusses the case of a sex scandal that involved President Clinton). For Meyrowitz, such 'fragility' is bound up with a broader questioning of authority in the age of electronic media.

So what problems might there be with Meyrowitz's understanding of place and with his argument that contemporary existence is increasingly placeless? From my perspective, there are five interconnected difficulties.

First, although Meyrowitz's observations on place as social position (on a transformation of the social order) do contain valuable insights, he tends to overestimate the degree of social change that has occurred. A good illustration of this overestimation is provided by his claim that: 'A telephone or computer in a ghetto tenement or in a suburban teenager's bedroom is potentially as effective as a telephone or computer in a corporate suite' (Meyrowitz, 1985, pp. 169–70). This claim clearly relates to his general contention that 'one may be in touch' in any location. Still, without wanting to underestimate the creative ingenuity of those living in ghetto tenements and suburban bedrooms, I doubt whether access to electronic media could, in itself, bring them social equality with corporate executives. Citing this particular claim of Meyrowitz's, Andrew Leyshon (1995, p. 33) is quite right to ask if technologically mediated communications are 'really as effective' for them 'in the way that Meyrowitz suggests': 'while the inner-city resident, the suburban teenager and the corporate executive may all be able to telephone a bank ... they would not all necessarily enjoy the privilege of being granted an audience with the bank manager'.

Second, Meyrowitz's account of social change is too much centred on media (a problem that, as a second-generation medium theorist, he inherits from McLuhan, whose account of human history is highly media-centric). While Meyrowitz (1985, p. 307) acknowledges in passing that 'change is always too complex to attribute to a single cause', his book seems to regard an 'evolution' in media as the principal motor of history. Initially, my criticism may appear to be an unusual one, because, like Meyrowitz, I am based in the broad field of media studies, and it might be assumed that anyone working in this field would automatically put media at the centre of their analyses. There is a difference, though, between studies that are 'media-oriented' and those that are 'media-centered' (Couldry, 2006, p. 13) in their investigations and explanations of social life. I think of my own work as falling into the former category. Of course, an appreciation of the distinctive features and affordances of media technologies within 'material culture' (Miller, 2010) is absolutely crucial, and I have a longstanding interest in studying everyday media uses (for example, see Moores, 2000), yet I firmly believe that these uses are best investigated in context, alongside other everyday practices and within wider social processes. I reject the sort of media-centric accounts that are found not only in medium theory but also in some areas of mainstream media theory. Indeed, David Morley (2007, p. 200) refers to my last book (Moores, 2005) as an instance of 'non-mediacentric ... media studies' (and the conclusion to my present book will extend this discussion of a non-media-centric approach).

Third, Meyrowitz's book tends to underestimate the ongoing significance of physical location. Scannell (1996, p. 141) points out that, given Meyrowitz's interest in television as a medium of communication, he has very little to say about 'the studio' as an important site for broadcasting. What I want to recall, though, is Meyrowitz's remark about 'physical isolation in specific locations', and here I come to the example that he gives of prisons and their inmates:

> The social meaning of a 'prison' ... has been changed as a result of electronic media of communication. ... The placement of prisoners in a secure, isolated location once led to both physical and informational separation from society. Today, however, many prisoners share with the larger society the privileges of radio, television, and telephone. ... For better or worse, those prisoners with access to electronic media are no longer completely segregated ... use of electronic media has led to a redefinition of the nature of 'imprisonment'.
>
> (Meyrowitz, 1985, pp. 117–18)

While it is true that many prisoners now have (limited) access to social information through electronic media, it strikes me that this is a rather strange example of the supposedly decreased significance of physical location in a 'relatively placeless' contemporary world. To state the obvious, prisoners remain under lock and key when they are accessing these technologies, and any minor 'redefinition of the nature of "imprisonment"' cannot hide the major fact that few people would ever choose to live in prison, precisely because it is a site of enforced 'physical isolation' from 'the larger society'. As Meyrowitz (ibid., p. 312) eventually concedes, 'regardless of media access, living in a ... prison cell ... and a middle class suburb are certainly not "equivalent" social experiences'. Interestingly, in his more recent work, he seems to alter his stance on place as physical location, admitting that 'the significance of locality persists even in the face of massive ... technological changes' (Meyrowitz, 2005, p. 21) and suggesting that electronically mediated communication 'may even enhance some aspects of connection to physical location' (ibid., p. 26). He argues that as the 'community of interaction' becomes a more 'mobile phenomenon' for many people, so choices about 'places to live' could well be of greater importance today: 'We increasingly choose our localities ... in terms of such variables as weather, architecture, quality of schools, density of population ... even "love at first sight"' (ibid.).

Fourth, continuing with the theme of place and location, might it not be possible and preferable to think of media settings or environments as 'places' of a sort, rather than equating the arrival of electronic media with the emergence of a placeless culture? There are odd occasions on which Meyrowitz does employ the term 'place' in this way. For example, early on in his book, he writes of how electronic media are 'bringing many different types of people to the same "place"' (Meyrowitz, 1985, p. 6; see also Adams, 1992, on television as 'gathering place'). This use of the word is compatible with Scannell's notes on the doubling of place, which I will be discussing in the next section of the chapter. Drawing on Scannell's book, *Radio, Television and Modern Life: A Phenomenological Approach* (1996), I want to argue that place, far from being marginalised, is instantaneously 'pluralised' in electronic media use. Indeed, this argument is, in my view, entirely compatible with Meyrowitz's own notes on the overlapping of physical settings and media settings.

Finally in this section, I want to signal what I see as a fifth difficulty with Meyrowitz's understanding of place, and it is a criticism that also applies, to some extent, to Scannell's employment of the term. The problem here is that it is not enough to conceptualise place as location, setting or environment (or even as social position). There is something more to place, and that something has to do with matters of 'dwelling' or 'habitation', which will be discussed in detail in the following chapter. For now, having mentioned those matters very briefly, let me leave this point undeveloped, because before I can deal with dwelling I need to extend my previous point about a 'pluralisation' of place.

The Doubling of Place

There are a number of similarities between the perspectives of Meyrowitz (1985) and Scannell (1996). Although Scannell does not cite McLuhan in his book, he shares with Meyrowitz an interest in the changing temporal and spatial arrangements of social life (see also Scannell, 2007, pp. 129–36, for his later assessment of McLuhan's medium theory). In addition, there is implicit agreement between them that media have an 'environmental' quality, since Scannell (1996, p. 8) writes of broadcasting's programme output that 'we find our way about in it' (I will be returning, later in the book, to the significance of knowing and finding 'our way about in' environments). Furthermore, Scannell's conceptual reference points do include Goffman's sociology, as well as other work in the tradition of micro-social theory (for example, in the areas known as 'ethnomethodology' and 'conversation analysis') where there is a persistent concern with the 'conditions of the intelligibility of the social practices of everyday existence' (ibid., p. 4). Other similarities between their perspectives include a shared interest in the 'sociable' features of electronically mediated encounters, and a common belief that media can be a democratising force in the contemporary world (but see Morley, 2000, pp. 108–12, for a critique of Scannell's position on 'sociability', in which Morley emphasises issues of social inequality and exclusion).

There are also notable differences between the views that Meyrowitz and Scannell have of electronic media (in Scannell's case, it is a perspective on the media of radio and television). One of these differences has to do with Scannell's 'phenomenological approach' to broadcasting, and, in particular, his engagement with some of Martin Heidegger's philosophical writings (see especially Heidegger, 1962). Meyrowitz refers in passing to sociologists who have been influenced, directly or indirectly, by phenomenological philosophy (Schutz, 1967; Garfinkel, 1984 [1967]; Berger and Luckmann, 1991 [1966]), positioning their work within the situationist tradition. However, phenomenology is not as central to his analytical framework as it is to Scannell's (see also Scannell, 1995). Scannell (1996, p. 149) identifies the 'dailiness' of broadcasting as its main 'organizing principle', and, drawing on Heideggerian terminology, he regards radio and television as 'equipment' providing 'an all-day everyday service that is ready-to-hand and available always anytime at the turn of a switch or the press of a button' (ibid., pp. 145–6; and see Blattner, 2006, pp. 49–52, for a helpful introductory commentary on Heidegger's notes on 'dealings' with equipment and on 'readiness-to-hand' in everyday living, in which Blattner considers the example of turning on music to listen to in his living room).

Interestingly, Heidegger's book, *Being and Time* (1962), which was originally published in German in the 1920s, includes a brief reflection on broadcasting. This is in the context of a wider philosophical discussion of what he calls 'the spatiality of being-in-the-world' (ibid., p. 138). There, Heidegger (ibid., p. 140) sees the newly arrived medium of radio as part of a 'push ... towards the conquest of remoteness' in contemporary society. Pursuing this line of thought, Scannell (1996, p. 173) explores the implications of radio and television use for listeners' and viewers' 'ways of being in the world', grounding his analysis in a social history of British broadcasting (Scannell's *Radio, Television and Modern Life* contains a fair amount of historical material, although the larger context for his analysis is furnished by an earlier, co-authored book on the history of the BBC, see Scannell and Cardiff, 1991).

The most notable difference between the perspectives of Meyrowitz and Scannell arises out of the latter theorist's exploration of changed 'ways of being', and it is here that I come to the doubling-of-place idea as an alternative to the no-sense-of-place thesis. Scannell (1996, p. 91) proposes that radio and television provide listeners and viewers with the 'magical' possibility 'of being in two places at once'. Broadcasting permits a witnessing of remote happenings that can take listeners and viewers as 'close' to those happenings, experientially, as they are to the goings-on in their physical environments. To repeat Heidegger's phrase, this is an element of 'the conquest of remoteness'. Things that were formerly 'far away' have become 'graspable' (ibid., p. 90). Indeed, in a striking parallel with Meyrowitz's remarks about the situational geography of social life, Scannell (ibid., p. 89) himself refers to the changing 'geography' of 'proximal experience' (more recently, another theorist to write on 'geographies of media and communication' is Adams, 2009, p. 185, who realises like Scannell that media, by 'bringing more places within the range of the senses', are enabling their users to ' "violate" the constraint that one can only be one place at a time').

Initially, the idea of doubling is developed in a chapter of Scannell's book that is concerned with broadcasting's occasional 'eventfulness'. Eventful occasions 'show up', as he puts it, against the 'backdrop' of 'broadcasting's daily output' (Scannell, 1996, p. 91). In a way that is usually anticipated and planned for, but sometimes unexpected, they punctuate the ordinary, largely uneventful character of radio and television in everyday living (see also Scannell, 1995; and Dayan and Katz, 1992, p. 5, who define 'media events' precisely as 'interruptions of routine' that 'intervene in the normal flow of broadcasting and our lives'). Scannell (1996, p. 84) sees, too, that in the 'broadcast coverage' of such an occasion:

> The liveness … is the key to its impact, since it offers the real sense of access to an event in its moment-by-moment unfolding. This presencing, this re-presenting of a present occasion to an absent audience, can … produce the effect of being-there, of being involved (caught up) in the here-and-now of the occasion.

Scannell's main examples of the coverage of eventful occasions are of BBC 'outside broadcasts' from British royal and state occasions, although he also points to the live coverage of major sports events (big football matches, horse races, tennis tournaments and so on), which form a part of the established 'broadcast year' or 'calendar' (ibid., p. 154). In fact, he ends the chapter on eventfulness with a highly personal account of his recollection of watching the climax of a golf tournament on television: 'Lyle holed out and became the first British golfer to win The Masters. I can see it, feel it, I am there, now, as I write. … It was an experience that I still own' (ibid., pp. 91–2).

Of course, there are significant differences between being physically present at an eventful occasion and 'being involved' or 'caught up' in an occasion as a television viewer. If these kinds of experience were exactly the same, then it would be difficult to explain why some people make a physical journey to 'be there' (even though, particularly in the case of sports events, they might well witness more of the action at home on television, see Brown, 1998). Still, Scannell's point is that there are effectively two events: 'there is the event-in-situ, and (at the same time) the event-as-broadcast' (Scannell, 1996, p. 79). He observes that:

> Public events now occur, simultaneously, in two different places: the place of the event itself and that in which it is watched and heard. Broadcasting mediates between these two sites. Events in public thus assume a degree of phenomenal complexity they did not hitherto possess.

> (ibid., p. 76)

Given the 'phenomenal complexity' of this doubling of place, Daniel Dayan and Elihu Katz (1992) ask whether it is appropriate to continue to think of events as wholly 'public' when they now 'take place', at least partly, in the 'private sphere'. These authors proceed to answer their own question by arguing that it is appropriate, because 'small groups congregated around the television set' are 'keenly aware that myriad other groups are doing likewise' (ibid., p. 146).

Having focused here on the way in which Scannell's idea of doubling is developed in his analysis of eventful occasions, I want to stress that there is no need to restrict its application to the study of eventfulness. What he calls the 'magic' of doubling is bound up more generally with 'the liveness of radio and television' that is also a part of broadcasting's dailiness, and, even in cases where programmes are routinely pre-recorded prior to the moment of their transmission, it remains a fundamental goal of the broadcasters to create a sense of temporal immediacy: 'the phenomenal now of broadcasting' (Scannell, 1996, p. 172). Indeed, I want to suggest that there is no need to restrict the use of his doubling-of-place idea to radio and television alone. It could be applied more widely, especially in studies of other electronic media, which share with broadcasting a capacity for 'liveness'. Clearly, there are important differences between radio, television, telephones and computers (despite the trend towards technological 'convergence'), yet these media of communication all 'afford' an instantaneous pluralisation of place.

As If We Knew Her Personally

In this section of my chapter and the two that follow it, I will be pursuing the argument about a doubling of place, making reference to some further examples. For now, my discussion remains focused on broadcasting (and also on eventfulness), but I will turn soon to other forms of electronically mediated communication in contexts of everyday living. Earlier in the chapter, I cited Turnock (2000), promising to come back to his work in due course. The moment to consider the research findings reported in his book has arrived, and it allows me to come back, too, to Horton and Wohl's concepts of the para-social relationship and mediated intimacy at a distance (Horton and Wohl, 1956).

Turnock's book presents an analysis of close to 300 solicited accounts, which were written by UK television viewers in the period shortly after the unexpected death of Princess Diana in 1997. These accounts describe viewers' personal experiences over the course of a week, starting with the breaking story of the car crash in which she died and finishing with the coverage of her funeral. As Turnock (2000, p. 4) states clearly at the outset, his book does not claim 'representativeness of a wider UK public', and he acknowledges that in the sample there was 'a bias towards an older, more middle-class demographic' as well as 'towards women'. However, as his analysis highlights, there is some fascinating empirical research material there on emotions following Princess Diana's death.

Turnock (ibid., pp. 13–14) observes that, as the story broke on UK television: 'Normal scheduling on the two main terrestrial channels ... was abandoned and the day was given over to live and continuous news. ... The non-stop coverage on BBC1 finally ended at 12.30am the following morning.' As with the eventful happenings of '9/11', just a few years later in 2001, the dailiness of broadcasting was unexpectedly disturbed (there was an abrupt interruption of routines). This disturbance or interruption intervened not only in 'the normal flow of broadcasting' but also in the flow of ordinary 'lives' (see Dayan and Katz, 1992, p. 5). For instance, one of the accounts quoted in Turnock (2000, p. 29) reads: 'We spent the whole day in the living room watching the news from 9.20am till 10.30pm. No one got dressed and everyone cried – even my Dad.'

The first kind of para-social relationship that Turnock deals with in his book, as he discusses people's accounts of the breaking story, is in the mediated quasi-interaction between newsreaders and viewers. He refers to one of the viewers who had sat through the 'live and continuous news', and who wrote of a particular BBC newsreader that 'he was there, serious, dependable ... I felt I needed him ... needed the television to stay with us all day' (ibid., p. 15). This is an example of what Turnock (ibid., p. 14) terms 'television as comforter' (even as the medium delivers troubling news from afar). Echoing Horton and Wohl's analysis, Turnock (ibid., p. 19) notes that 'the face-to-camera address of the news presenter re-creates that ... important social experience – the face-to-face encounter', and he goes on to suggest that newsreaders can come to be regarded by some viewers as 'trusted friends' (this clearly echoes Meyrowitz, 1985, p. 120, on 'para-social friends').

In these eventful circumstances, the other non-reciprocal relationship of intimacy at a distance was, of course, the emotional connection with Princess Diana experienced by those viewers who mourned her death. Turnock (2000, p. 35) asks the key question here: 'How is it possible to grieve over someone that you have never met?' The answer is to be found in extracts from the written accounts such as 'we knew so much about this woman and had seen so much of her that it was as if we knew her personally', and: 'She had seemed so much part of our lives for almost 20 years ... I have to admit feeling quite a profound sense of loss' (ibid., p. 47). Although it was rare for Princess Diana to look straight to the television camera and use 'the mode of direct address' (Horton and Wohl, 1956, p. 215) as presenters do, she made frequent media appearances during the period following her engagement to Prince Charles (Dayan and Katz, 1992, take the live broadcast coverage of the wedding as one of their case studies). She came to occupy an extraordinary social position through her marriage into the British royal family, and yet, in media settings, she often gave a 'performance of "ordinariness"' (Couldry, 2001, p. 231). According to Turnock (2000, p. 47), then, 'Diana was very much like a regular cast member in a television serial', who offered 'melodramatic identifications' (Ang, 1996 [1990]) to viewers as she went through the 'ups and downs' (Turnock, 2000, p. 45) of life.

Let me come now to Turnock's chapter on the funeral, because the following account from a viewer provides a clear illustration of what Scannell (1996) calls the doubling of place:

> My family and I watched the entire funeral. My husband has his own business, but he was shut for the day as a mark of respect ... we just felt it was the appropriate thing to do. At times it was difficult because we have a thirteen-month-old baby and sometimes he got bored, so we took it in turns to entertain him. We watched BBC1 until she reached her final resting place around 2.15 pm. We stayed

at home in our breakfast room, drinking tea and crying. It did not
feel right to go out on such a sad day.

(Turnock, 2000, p. 99)

Once again, as with the household that 'spent the whole day ... watching the news' a few days earlier, there is the strong sense of a break with
routine. The husband's business is 'shut for the day', the family stays in
the 'breakfast room' until well into the afternoon, and nobody goes out
of the house. Once again, too, there are tears shed (melodramatic identifications are experienced corporeally and affectively), suggesting the
'profound sense of loss'. Crucially, though, there is a dual sense of being
involved or caught up in the remote happenings, 'until she reached her
final resting place', while also congregating in a small group 'around the
television set', in a domestic context with its associated distractions
(entertaining a child).

There are two final, brief points that I want to make in this section.
The first of these has to do with what Scannell terms the phenomenal
complexity of public events today. The complexity that he was referring
to is in the simultaneous existence of 'the event-in-situ' and 'the event-
as-broadcast' (Scannell, 1996, p. 79), with the event-as-broadcast being
experienced by 'myriad ... groups' (Dayan and Katz, 1992, p. 146) across
dispersed sites of use. In the case of Princess Diana's funeral, though,
things are more complex still, because those mourners who had trav-
elled to central London to gather in large numbers outside Westminster
Abbey (the location for the event-in-situ) were able to watch the service
being relayed live on outdoor screens. This rather peculiar 'mixture of
different forms of interaction' (Thompson, 1995, p. 85) involved an
element of physically 'being there', locally co-present with others in a
crowd, but it also involved the electronically mediated communication
of a television broadcast. My second point here is concerned with the
geographical scale of the event-as-broadcast. Although the empirical
research material analysed by Turnock came solely from the UK, and
while Scannell's main examples of eventful occasions are national ones,
coverage of Princess Diana's funeral had a transnational reach (for a
fuller consideration of 'media events in a global age', see Couldry *et al.*,
2010). For example, Jean Duruz and Carol Johnson (1999) discuss what
they call 'mourning at a distance' in Australia, referring to reports of
empty Melbourne nightclubs at the time that the funeral was broadcast
live. Interestingly, they also quote an Australian journalist who wrote of
Princess Diana: 'I didn't know her ... but like the rest of the world I felt
I did' (ibid., p. 149).

There Are Two Theres There

In this section, I discuss the doubling or pluralisation of place in electronically mediated communications via the telephone, and my main example here concerns mobile-phone use. There is now a sizeable body of academic literature on the mobile phone, sometimes called the 'cell phone' (for instance, Katz and Aakhus, 2002; Ling, 2004; Nyíri, 2005; Goggin, 2006; Horst and Miller, 2006; Katz, 2006; Castells *et al.*, 2007; Goggin, 2008; Green and Haddon, 2009; Ling and Donner, 2009), and many authors have discussed the implications of mobile-phone use for the temporal and spatial organisation of everyday living. For example, Rich Ling's work addresses, among other things, a transformation that he terms the 'softening of schedules' (Ling, 2004, pp. 73–6), exploring the 'micro-coordination' of physical movements and 'daily interactions' by mobile-phone users (see especially Ling and Donner, 2009, pp. 91–4). The focus of my discussion, though, will be on an illustration of doubling that appears in the work of a micro-social theorist and conversation analyst, Emanuel Schegloff (2002).

Schegloff (ibid., pp. 285–6) offers the following story, which is 'set' on a train carriage in New York and also, to be precise, in a media environment of 'talk-in-interaction':

> A young woman is talking on the cell phone, apparently to her boyfriend, with whom she is in something of a crisis. Her voice projects in far-from-dulcet tones. Most of the passengers take up a physical and postural stance of busying themselves with other foci of attention (their reading matter, the scene passing by the train's windows, etc.), busy doing 'not overhearing this conversation' ... except for one passenger. And when the protagonist of this tale has her eyes intersect this fellow-passenger's gaze, she calls out in outraged protest, 'Do you mind?! This is a private conversation!'

Although Schegloff (ibid.) does not cite Scannell's work on broadcasting (I assume that he was unaware of it), there is a remarkable echo of the doubling-of-place idea in Schegloff's own commentary on this story of mobile-phone use. The young woman who is 'the protagonist of this tale' is, in his words, 'in two places at the same time – and the railroad car is only one of them' (ibid., p. 286). 'The other place that she is', he explains, 'is "on the telephone" ... there are two "theres" there' (ibid., pp. 286–7). Interestingly, when writing on the notion of being 'in two places at the same time', he also points to the 'two "theres" there' in everyday uses of small, portable music players such as the 'Walkman', where an individual is simultaneously moving around 'in public places – on campus, in buses ... on sidewalks' and 'in an auditory environment pulsating with sounds' (ibid.; and for empirical research findings on 'personal stereo' and 'iPod' use in urban environments, see especially Bull, 2000, 2007).

The tale that Schegloff tells is one in which there are plural and competing 'definitions of situations' (Meyrowitz, 1985, p. 24). There is intended humour in the story, and this relates to the young woman's insistence that she is having 'a private conversation' (an interpersonal encounter in a media setting), despite the fact that her 'far-from-dulcet tones' are clearly audible to other passengers in the train carriage (a physical setting shared with strangers). Still, Schegloff (2002, p. 286) acknowledges that the protagonist may, at least implicitly, 'understand ... "on the telephone" ... to be a private place', and he does identify reasons for her assertion to be supported: 'this young woman is talking to her boyfriend, about intimate matters, in the usual conversational manner – except for the argumentative mode, and this also, perhaps especially, makes it a private conversation'. Indeed, that 'definition of the situation' is supported in a way by almost all of her fellow passengers. The carriage is 'a place full of overhearers', but they are 'pretending not to hear' (ibid.). They look down at their books, newspapers and magazines, or else out at 'the scene passing by', but above all they avoid any eye contact with the woman on the mobile phone. In ethnomethodological terms, they are, as Schegloff puts it, 'doing' not overhearing one side of the conversation. However, there is then the single passenger who refuses to accept this collaboratively performed pretence, perhaps as a result of being irritated by the intrusion of private talk into a public space. At the moment when that passenger's gaze meets the look of the protagonist, the different situational definitions come into conflict with one another.

I like Schegloff's story because it highlights a specific, evidently dramatic case of the overlapping or 'intersection' (ibid.) of physical and media environments (of what he calls the two 'theres' there). It helps to reinforce my more general argument, which has been progressively developed in this chapter, that analyses of social interactions and experiences in contemporary living need to be sensitive to such doublings and intersections. Another helpful illustration of the pluralising of settings in telephone use can be found in Deborah Cameron's discussion of the labour that is performed in 'call centres' (Cameron, 2000). Her study brings home the importance of workplace contexts for what is being said by the employees in their conversations with customers. These workers, then, are not simply 'on the telephone'. There is an overlapping 'there', which is the social setting of the call centre, and in this context their performance is subject to various sorts of training, target-setting and surveillance (see also Aneesh, 2006, p. 93, for a further twist on call centres, since he considers the case of nightshift workers in India who are engaged in a 'virtual migration', talking 'with friendly voices, American pseudonyms, and ... an American accent' to customers in the US).

Continuous Social Spaces

Finally in this chapter, I turn my attention to some academic literature on internet use that is also concerned with 'intersecting' environments in the changing situational geography of social life. A good example to start with here is the 'ethnographic approach' to the internet advocated by Daniel Miller and Don Slater (2000), an anthropologist and a sociologist respectively. They position their work within a second generation of internet research, distinguishing what they do from an 'earlier generation of ... writing that ... focused on the way in which ... new media seemed able to constitute spaces or places apart from the rest of social life' (ibid., p. 4). Rather than thinking of online settings as having a kind of 'self-enclosed cyberian apartness', they choose, instead, to treat these media environments 'as continuous with ... other social spaces' (ibid., p. 5). 'That is to say', explain Miller and Slater (ibid., p. 7), 'these spaces are important as part of everyday life.'

In their own ethnographic research, Miller and Slater explore varied uses of the internet by people who are physically located on the Caribbean island of Trinidad. Reflecting on their findings, they note that:

> The notion of cyberspace as a place apart from offline life would lead us to expect to observe a process in which participants are abstracted and distanced from local and embodied social relations, for example becoming less explicitly Trinidadian. We found utterly the opposite. Trinidadians ... invest much energy in trying to make online life as Trinidadian as they can make it ... a place to perform Trini-ness.
>
> (ibid.)

For example, the researchers consider an everyday social activity known as 'liming'. This word has traditionally been employed by Trinidadians to describe a specific form of talk or 'banter' that is associated with 'hanging out' on the streetcorner or in the 'rumshop' ('a local, down-market drinking place'), but Miller and Slater (ibid., p. 89) report that, in addition, ' "liming" was the word ... used to describe chatting online'. Mediated encounters in certain internet 'chat rooms', then, have come 'to be seen ... as liming extended to ... another social space' (ibid.). Those 'rooms' are accessed, too, by Trinidadians who are physically absent from the island, living in other parts of the world (see also Miller, 2010, pp. 114–18, for a retrospective commentary on the work that he did with Slater on the 'Trinidadian Internet', in which Miller makes the further, valuable point that 'being Trini' is not simply a fixed category of identity that remains untouched by practices of internet use).

Of course, it is important to acknowledge that there are some internet users who do go online in order to experiment with their presentation of self in spaces they understand to be 'apart from the rest of social life' (a classic investigation of this sort of 'identity play' is Turkle, 1996a). However, even in such circumstances, 'to the extent that some people may actually treat various Internet relations as "a world apart" ... this is something that needs to be socially explained' (Miller and Slater, 2000, p. 5). It is therefore necessary to ask why an 'escape' from everyday living might be sought in the first instance, and how different online identities still relate in particular ways to offline selves (to be fair, Turkle is one of the earlier generation of internet researchers who looks to provide answers to these questions in her empirical case studies; see also Turkle, 1996b).

Sociologist Lori Kendall (2002) reports the findings of her ethnographic research on the users of an internet forum that she describes as a 'virtual pub', and while she points there to rare cases of online experimentation with identity (to playful 'gender switching', for example), she finds that, for the most part, the forum offers its participants 'another social space' (Miller and Slater, 2000, p. 89) into which they can extend their offline activities and interests. Much of the 'talk' in this forum, then, is between men who are employed in the computer industry in the US, and Kendall (2002, p. 73) observes that their online conversations often 'revolve around computers, including discussions of new software, planned purchases, and technical advice'. Furthermore, there have been 'informal offline gatherings' of participants 'in the San Francisco Bay Area and elsewhere' (ibid., p. 19), some of which she attended as part of her ethnographic research, and regulars at those gatherings had knowledge of each other based on face-to-face meetings as well as on technologically mediated interactions.

I want to stress here that one of Kendall's main concerns is precisely with the doublings and intersections of online and offline spaces. Like Miller and Slater, she is opposed to 'viewing cyberspace as a separate sovereign world' (ibid., p. 8) and she seeks to understand how users are 'weaving online communications ... into their existing offline lives' (ibid., p. 16). Indeed, in the opening chapter of her book, she gives the following account of her own routine when logged onto the internet 'for long periods':

> I frequently leave the computer to get food, go to the bathroom, or respond to someone in the physical room in which I'm sitting. If the text appearing on my screen slows to a crawl or the conversation ceases to interest me, I may cast about for something else offline to engage me.
>
> (ibid., p. 7)

Kendall (ibid., pp. 7–8) proceeds to state that, although the virtual pub in her study 'provides for me a feeling of being in a place, that place in some sense overlays ... physical space'. She tells this rather mundane, personal story as a way of emphasising the point that no one 'inhabits only cyberspace' (ibid., p. 8), since there are always, simultaneously, 'two ... places' in internet use.

Kendall's personal story, which, if the word 'computer' was replaced by 'TV', could pass as an account of distracted, domestic television viewing (see Morley, 1986, 1992), connects well with the call from Miller and Slater (2000, p. 7) for the internet to be considered 'as part of everyday life'. A similar call is made by Caroline Haythornthwaite and Barry Wellman (2002) in the introduction to their edited book, *The Internet in Everyday Life* (Wellman and Haythornthwaite, 2002). They describe that book as 'a harbinger of a new way of thinking about the Internet: not as a special system but as routinely incorporated into everyday life' (Haythornthwaite and Wellman, 2002, p. 6), and, positioning this work within the new generation of internet research, they look to distinguish it from what they call 'the many books and articles about cyber-this and cyber-that'. Topics covered by their contributors include, for instance, the everyday practices of distance learners, 'teleworkers' and online shoppers.

A helpful way of theorising how media technologies are 'routinely incorporated into everyday life' is through the concept of 'domestication' (see especially Silverstone *et al.*, 1992; Silverstone, 1994, p. 174; also Berker *et al.*, 2006). I will bring the section and the chapter to a close now by referring briefly to two ethnographic studies (Lally, 2002; Bakardjieva, 2005), carried out in Australia and Canada respectively, which have each employed this concept in analysing the uses of 'home computers' in household contexts. Elaine Lally's analysis emerged out of her interviews and observations in over thirty computer-owning households in the Sydney area, and her main interest is in understanding how mass-produced commodities can come to be experienced as personal possessions as they get integrated into people's domestic lives (Lally, 2002). She advances the argument that home computers, prior to the moment of purchase, have already been through a process of 'pre-domestication' (ibid., p. 54; see also Silverstone and Haddon, 1996) at the stages of design and advertising, as they get styled and marketed for household use. However, Lally's focus is on the post-purchase integration of these commodities, via household members' varied and sometimes contested ways of making themselves 'at home'. It is through such a process that computers are ultimately 'domesticated'. They are positioned within a 'domestic ecology of objects', becoming an element of 'the familiarity ... of the material environment' (Lally, 2002, p. 169) in households (these themes of 'familiarity' and 'at-homeness' will be central to my discussion in the next chapter). Maria Bakardjieva (2005) presents related findings on the practices of 'making room' for home computers in everyday living. She refers, in a remarkably similar way, to the 'integration of a new artefact into ... the patterns of spatial differentiation in a household' (ibid., p. 139). Offering detailed ethnographic portraits of selected people with domestic internet access in Vancouver, Bakardjieva (ibid., pp. 140–56) identifies several specific ways in which this social and spatial 'integration of a new artefact' is accomplished (see her accounts of 'the wired basement', 'the family computer room' and so on). In addition, her book contains interesting empirical research findings on users' activities in those online environments that 'overlay' the physical settings of households. For example, she discusses the sociability of internet 'chatting' and participation in various 'news-groups'. Significantly, though, Bakardjieva seeks to contextualise her findings on 'virtual togetherness' by linking them to an understanding of people's offline circumstances.

2 When Space Feels Thoroughly Familiar

Having established certain ideas about the changing situational geography of social life, I want to come back now to a point that I left undeveloped in the previous chapter. In my sympathetic critique of Joshua Meyrowitz's *No Sense of Place* (1985), the last of my five difficulties with his understanding of place was that it fails to deal with what I referred to there, rather mysteriously, as a 'something more'. I hinted that this 'something more to place' has to do with matters of dwelling or habitation, requiring definitions of place as location to be extended significantly. In order to develop my point, it is necessary for me to explain in detail what these matters are, and the explanation that I offer in the current chapter involves venturing well beyond what would normally be regarded as the boundaries of media studies. Much of the academic literature that I will be engaging with is to be found in the disciplines of geography, philosophy, anthropology and sociology. The main focus of this work is not usually on media of communication and their applications in contemporary society, and when media do figure they are not always theorised in a way that I find helpful. For instance, problematic claims about placelessness resurface towards the end of the chapter. Nevertheless, I want to insist that the literature I will be reviewing is of the utmost relevance for the analysis of media uses, and for an appreciation of how everyday physical and media environments become 'lived' or 'inhabited' spaces. A link with part of the previous chapter (where I referred to Heidegger, 1962; Scannell, 1995, 1996) is provided by my emphasis over the coming pages on phenomenological perspectives.

Space and Place

The words in the title of this second chapter are taken from Yi-Fu Tuan's book, *Space and Place: The Perspective of Experience* (1977), which has been described recently by Tim Cresswell (2008, p. 53) as 'a classic text' in human geography (see also Rodaway, 2004, for a profile of Tuan as a key thinker on space and place). Tuan is perhaps the best known of a number of geographers who were developing, during the 1970s in North America, a distinctive 'experiential perspective' on formations of place in everyday living (for example, see Buttimer, 1976; Seamon, 1979; Buttimer and Seamon, 1980; Relph, 2008 [1976]). These geographers drew on, among other influences, the insights of European phenomenological philosophy (see especially Heidegger, 1962, 1993 [1971]; Bachelard, 1969; Merleau-Ponty, 2002 [1962]). As Cresswell (2008, p. 55) observes, the themes opened up by Tuan (1977) (and by his fellow pioneers) foreshadowed 'much of the most exciting work in the contemporary social sciences and humanities' (I will be referring to some examples of that contemporary work in due course, as well as to some of the older philosophical foundations of what Seamon, 1980, p. 148, labels 'phenomenological geography').

In an article by Tuan (1996a [1974], p. 445) with the same title as his subsequent book, in which he began to set out his conceptualisations of space and place, he states clearly that: 'Place ... is more than location.' Interestingly, with regard to Meyrowitz's dual definition of place, Tuan (ibid.) notes, too, that it is more than 'one's position in society' (although issues of social difference and power remain important for an understanding of place). For him, the something more to place has to do precisely with matters of dwelling or habitation, because he argues that place is constituted when locations are routinely lived-in and when what he calls a 'habit field' or a 'field of care' (ibid., pp. 451–2) is formed. With reference to physical settings, he argues that place is accomplished through repetitive, habitual practices (see Heidegger, 1993 [1971], p. 349, on dwelling as 'from the outset "habitual"'), giving rise to 'affective' attachments in which 'people are emotionally bound to their material environment' (Tuan, 1996a [1974], pp. 451–2).

It is just such a definition of place (as an experiential accomplishment binding people and environments) that is missing from Meyrowitz's understanding of the term (Meyrowitz, 1985). Indeed, it is only implicit in Paddy Scannell's phenomenology of radio and television (Scannell, 1995, 1996; however, I anticipate a further development of his phenomenological perspective in Scannell, forthcoming). Scannell's identification of broadcasting's dailiness and readiness-to-hand is extremely valuable, as is his notion that people can find their way about in its programme output. As I showed in the previous chapter, he also points to how listeners and viewers may get caught up in momentous public occasions, and to the implications of radio and television consumption for ways of being-in-the-world. Still, the fact remains that in his *Radio, Television and Modern Life* (Scannell, 1996) the doubling-of-place idea remains one in which place is conceptualised primarily as a location, rather than as a practical and emotional accomplishment. The doubling of place is understood, then, as a simultaneous 'occupation' of two different yet continuous social spaces. For this reason, I see the writings of Tuan, and of others in human geography and elsewhere who broadly share a focus on the experiential dimension of place (on issues of habit, affect and attachment to environment in everyday living), as crucially important for my book's overall thesis, because they move beyond observing the occupation of space to deal with its inhabiting.

Tuan (1977), as his book's title suggests, distinguishes the term 'space' from place, equating the former with physical location (although, as Casey, 2002, p. 404, rightly cautions, this must not lead to thinking of space as a 'raw' material that is 'simply there', and that is 'coterminous with nature'). Space, writes Tuan (1977, p. 6), 'becomes place as we get to know it better and endow it with value'. Place, for him (ibid., p. 73), is location made familiar, concrete and meaningful through practice: 'When space feels thoroughly familiar ... it has become place.' The kind of 'practice' that he is concerned with here requires a 'learning' process, but it is not necessarily the type of learning that is associated with 'formal instruction', as it tends to be bound up with the apparently unremarkable business of 'getting around' and 'orientation' in everyday environments:

> We are in a strange part of town: unknown space stretches ahead of us. In time we know a few landmarks and the routes connecting them. Eventually what was strange town ... becomes familiar place. Abstract space, lacking significance other than strangeness, becomes concrete place, filled with meaning ... we are oriented ... we can find our way.
>
> (ibid., p. 199)

However, Tuan (ibid., p. 68) realises that the ordinary practices of 'wayfinding' referred to in his example, which serve to transform initially 'unknown' locations into places, might not be straightforwardly translatable into words or pictures: 'People who are good at finding their way in the city may be poor at giving street directions to the lost, and hopeless in their attempts to draw maps.' What he names 'environmental experience' (ibid., p. v; also a central term for Seamon, 1979, whose research will be discussed later) can often be difficult to express symbolically. This is because the 'know-how' required to get around with ease in urban spaces, and to feel at home in everyday environments more generally, is practical and embodied. In addition, it is important to note that a 'sense of place' (Tuan, 1996a [1974], p. 446), which emerges when 'we are oriented', involves a combination of bodily senses.

One of Tuan's main arguments is that place 'exists at different scales' (Tuan, 1977, p. 149; see also Tuan, 1996a [1974], p. 455). In the example that I have just cited, his interest is in formations of place in the context of city neighbourhoods. At the larger scale of the region or nation, he is concerned with feelings of 'attachment to homeland' (Tuan, 1977, p. 149; and see Edensor, 2002, pp. 88–98, for an account of how routine activities or 'habitual performances', including ritually tuning in to scheduled broadcast programmes, can be significant for formations of collective identity). On a different level, Tuan (1996a [1974], p. 455) contends that: 'Place can be as small as the corner of a room'. At this micro-social scale, for instance, 'a favorite armchair is a place' (Tuan, 1977, p. 149). Indeed, following in the footsteps of Gaston Bachelard (1969), whose book, *The Poetics of Space*, is a classic philosophical study of the significance of domestic settings, Tuan (1977, p. 144) writes about 'the house as home' (see also Heidegger, 1993 [1971], p. 348, who gives a valuable reminder that 'houses in themselves' do not 'hold any guarantee that dwelling occurs in them'). Tuan (1977, p. 144) remarks that the house as home is 'full of ordinary objects', which are known intimately and sensually 'through use': 'They are almost a part of ourselves.' This point about a household's 'ordinary objects' that are 'almost a part of ourselves' reminds me of Elaine Lally's analysis of the domestication of the home computer (Lally, 2002), discussed at the end of my previous chapter, in which she refers to the integration of the commodity into an 'ecology of objects'. It enables me to signal the way forward, too, to a later stage in the current chapter, when I will be considering 'embodiment relations' (Ihde, 1990, p. 74) involving the uses of media technologies within familiar material environments.

Again and Again

Many years after the publication of *Space and Place* (Tuan, 1977), Tuan (2004) wrote a piece on senses of place that I find particularly interesting for its examples of attachment to what I would call, following Meyrowitz's lead, media environments (Meyrowitz, 1985), although I should make it clear that Tuan does not employ this term in his work. In the piece I am referring to, he picks up the theme of time and place that had been explored towards the end of *Space and Place*, where Tuan (1977, p. 202) asks how long it takes for people 'to form a lasting attachment' to a location. He does acknowledge the potential for occasional cases of 'love at first sight' (Tuan, 2004, p. 48; and see again Meyrowitz, 2005, p. 26), but, in his reflections on time and place, he emphasises the importance of repetition and return.

Describing the routine physical movements of everyday living, Tuan (1977, p. 180) notes that these often 'complete a more or less circular path'. For example:

> In the home pieces of furniture such as a desk, an armchair, the kitchen sink ... are points along a complex path of movement that is followed day after day. ... As a result of habitual use the path ... acquires a density of meaning. ... The path and the pauses along it constitute a ... place.
>
> (ibid., pp. 180–2)

There might also be everyday movements that 'swing back and forth like a pendulum' (ibid., p. 180), such as those involved in commuting between a private house or apartment and a public site of work. Whether it is a cyclical or a pendulum-like motion, though, Tuan's concern is with repetitive, habitual practices that are performed 'day after day', which serve to 'constitute' places over lengthy periods of immersion in environments.

In *Space and Place*, Tuan barely mentions media of communication and their applications in contemporary society. However, in the more recent piece of his that I want to consider now, there is a fascinating discussion of affective attachments to 'photographs', 'movies', 'stories and novels' and 'music' (Tuan, 2004, pp. 49–53). What he highlights in this discussion is the significance of their repeated use (of returning to them 'again and again', see ibid., p. 51).

When writing on photographs, then, Tuan (ibid., p. 50) states that it is possible to 'develop the habit of dwelling imaginatively' in particular images, which 'we ... visit and revisit' (it is worth adding here that such engagements with photographs are not only visual, since the images have traditionally been physical or material things that are handled, and today they are often accessed on screen by pressing a button or double-clicking a mouse). Similarly, when attending to the example of cinema, he makes the following personal 'confession':

I have seen the movie *Gone With the Wind* at least a dozen times, the first time ... when I was a child. ... I returned to the movie again and again. For, after several viewings, *Gone With the Wind* became a place for me.

(ibid., p. 51)

The last few words of that quote ('became a place for me') are pivotal, because Tuan is clearly thinking about place as an experiential accomplishment, as 'more than location'. A specific media environment, in this instance a film, is transformed through repeated use into a 'lived space' (the notion of 'space as ... lived ... the space of "inhabitants" and "users"' comes from Lefebvre, 1991, p. 39; see also Cresswell, 2008, pp. 57–8, who asserts that this idea of an 'inhabited space' is 'very close to Tuan's definition of place'). Indeed, given the availability of audiovisual recording and playback facilities today, repeat viewings of films are now common, and it is even possible for viewers to select their favourite scenes from a movie to watch again and again.

Tuan's next example is that of oral and print fictions. He observes how 'young children ... like to hear the same story over and over', and also how some 'adults ... revisit ... favorite novels' rather like they might revisit a 'hometown' (Tuan, 2004, p. 52). Although the narrative 'paths' will already be 'well trodden' by such hearers or readers, who are well aware of how the stories conclude, they nevertheless return to them precisely for the evocation of a familiar fictional world. Finally for Tuan, there is the experience of listening to music, and the intriguing question of why some people return again and again to their favourite musical pieces. He insists that they are not doing so in order to hear and be moved by 'something new' every time they listen to such a piece. Rather, they do so in order 'to be exposed to a presence, to be in the midst of a magical place' (ibid., p. 53; and note that there are echoes of Scannell, 1996, with this reference to 'presencing' and the magical).

From my perspective, it is a pity that Tuan does not extend his insightful analysis, so as to include experiences of other media environments. It is also a pity that, in his discussion of photography, cinema, fiction and music, he chooses to employ a ranking of different types of place. In this ranking, valued physical settings are privileged while meaningful media settings are relegated to the status of 'surrogate place' (Tuan, 2004, p. 49), or are seen as mere 'cousins to place' (ibid., p. 52). Personally, I see no reason why any universal hierarchy of place-types is required. Nevertheless, I want to argue that Tuan's general approach is potentially a fruitful one for those who work in media studies, with wider applications than he seems to realise. For example, his emphasis on the importance of repetition and return for the constitution of places could help to throw some new light on the uses of an 'everyday mass medium' such as the newspaper. Consider the regular readers of a daily paper. It would be reasonable to assume that these readers are expecting to find something new every time they buy the paper, since they do so partly on the promise of 'news'. However, it is worth noting that another, possibly more significant, element of their engagement with and attachment to the paper is likely to be the expectation of finding the same things 'over and over', day after day. The paper's layout, then, tends to be unchanging, which can be a source of comfort for readers. They are presumably able to 'get around' in this media environment with ease, physically turning the pages with their fingers, having developed the necessary know-how to find their way quickly to the entertainment section, the sports pages and so on. They may also get to know, over time, the styles of particular journalists and personalities who write for the paper on a regular basis. If Tuan was to extend his analysis in the direction I am advocating here, he might well conclude that the paper is a location or a setting that can be transformed into a place through 'habitual use' (that is, made concrete and meaningful through practice). As a habit field or a field of care is formed, the space of the daily paper comes to feel 'thoroughly familiar'.

In relation to my proposal that the daily paper might become a place for its readers, according to Tuan's definition of the term, I will bring the present section of the chapter to a close now with a final point, concerning the connections between newspapers, radio and television as media of communication. I find it interesting that Scannell (1996) mentions these connections, occasionally and just briefly, in his *Radio, Television and Modern Life*. While there are evidently many differences between print and electronic media, he observes that 'the press and broadcasting' (sometimes referred to, collectively, simply as 'the media') have a comparable 'everyday worldliness' (ibid., p. 177) and share similar principles of 'serial production' (ibid., p. 10). Both 'provide a daily service' that is the remarkable outcome of a complex, ongoing industrial process, yet they each manage to do so 'in such a way that it appears as no more than what I ... am entitled to expect as an aspect of my days' (ibid., p. 149), or, putting it more colloquially, 'as "no big deal" ' (ibid., p. 177). It follows from this comparison that it is also possible to understand the routine uses of broadcasting as place-constituting activities. The media spaces or environments made available by radio and television may, over time, come to feel thoroughly familiar too.

Walking/Driving in the City

At this stage in the chapter, I want to return to the matter of getting around in urban physical environments, which was raised by Tuan (1977) in his illustration of the distinction between space and place. This is because it enables me to link Tuan's important remarks about orientation and wayfinding with the work of another theorist who was writing on a similar theme during the 1970s, but on the other side of the Atlantic. I am thinking here of Michel de Certeau's book, *The Practice of Everyday Life* (1984), which was published in English a decade after it originally appeared in French (for an early discussion and application of his ideas within media studies, see Silverstone, 1989). In particular, I am thinking about a chapter of de Certeau's book on 'walking in the city' (de Certeau, 1984, pp. 91–110; see also de Certeau, 1985), on which I will be focusing initially in the present section. I then want to make a further link, this time with Nigel Thrift's work in contemporary human geography, which goes under the name of 'non-representational theory' (see especially Thrift, 2007). Later in the section, I turn to his account of 'driving in the city' (see ibid., pp. 75–88, for material that was first published as Thrift, 2004a; and see Amin and Thrift, 2002, pp. 100–1). In the course of considering these reflections by de Certeau and Thrift, I will also be referring, along the way, to some interesting work on the significance of media technologies in practices of walking/driving in the city.

De Certeau's discussion of 'the city' begins with a personal story of an eventful experience. He describes how, on a visit to the US, he viewed New York 'from the 110th floor of the World Trade Center' (de Certeau, 1984, p. 91; that particular perspective is no longer available, of course, following the tragic events of 9/11). This experience of 'elevation', he argues, has granted people the extraordinary opportunity of 'looking down like a god', as if at a map, on a city that is 'immobilized before the eyes' (ibid., pp. 91–2). Meanwhile, writes de Certeau (ibid., p. 93), 'ordinary practitioners of the city live "down below" … they are walkers'. Their everyday practices of 'moving about' (ibid., p. xix) are a crucial part of the 'mobility characteristic of the bustling city' (ibid., p. 93), which can be contrasted with the map-like city that is seen from up high. It is 'on ground level', then, that the 'footsteps' and 'intertwined paths' of walkers help to constitute, collectively, what Tuan would call places: 'a process of appropriation of the topographical system on the part of the pedestrian' (ibid., p. 97).

Elaborating on that contrast between 'the planned city' ('immobilized' from above) and 'the mobile city' ('bustling' with human bodily activity on the streets 'down below') (ibid., p. 110), de Certeau borrows selected concepts from the discipline of linguistics. At the time he was writing *The Practice of Everyday Life*, he was certainly not alone in drawing on ideas from that discipline, as there had been a broader 'linguistic turn' in the social sciences and humanities, which was mainly associated with a movement known as 'structuralism'. However, what is interesting about de Certeau's appropriation of linguistics for social theory is his emphasis on language use in context, 'the act of speaking (or practice of language) ... in relation to its circumstances' (ibid., p. 33), rather than on abstract structures of language. As he points out, this is the concern of a branch of linguistics called 'pragmatics' (ibid.; in a different way, it is also the concern of conversation analysis in sociology, see Sacks, 1995), and it is therefore possible to think of his book as developing a sort of pragmatics of everyday living. For instance, in his chapter on walking in the city, he writes of 'pedestrian speech acts' (de Certeau, 1984, p. 97) or 'pedestrian enunciation' (ibid., p. 99), arguing that 'walking is to the urban system what the speech act is to language' (ibid., p. 97) as a structure or sign-system. In other words, de Certeau's interest is in how the routine physical movements of pedestrians serve to 'articulate' cities, creating 'another "spatiality"' by turning urban settings into inhabited spaces: 'Thus the street geometrically defined by urban planning is transformed ... by walkers' (ibid., p. 117).

Although Tuan (1977) does not draw on linguistics in the same way as de Certeau (and while reading de Certeau, 1984, alongside Tuan can be a little confusing, because the terms space and place are employed there in a way that turns the usual conceptual distinction in geography 'on its head', Cresswell, 2004, p. 38), I am nevertheless struck by the parallels between their approaches. Both theorists are concerned with ordinary activities of getting around. Both are concerned with experiential accomplishments that bind people and environments. However, one significant difference between them has to do with de Certeau's connecting of the pragmatics and the politics of everyday living. For me, this connection is simultaneously valuable and problematic. It is valuable because it raises issues of social difference and power (about which I will have more to say later) that are important when considering routine practices, but it is also problematic because, in the specific case of de Certeau's work, rather too simple an opposition is set up between the 'clever tricks of the "weak"' and the 'order established by the "strong"' (de Certeau, 1984, p. 40). Within the terms of that general opposition between the 'weak' and the 'strong' in contemporary society, pedestrian movements, alongside a range of other practices such as 'talking, reading ... cooking, etc.', are understood by de Certeau (ibid., p. xix) to be creative improvisations that are 'tactical in character', and he contends that these tactical 'ways of using' involve a contestation of the 'dominant ... order' (ibid., p. xiii). It is not difficult to see that, while his attention to the improvisational aspects of quotidian cultures is to be welcomed, such a model of resistance relies upon a highly romanticised view of ordinary activities (see also Fiske, 1989, for a similarly romanticised view). Indeed, *The Practice of Everyday Life* begins, tellingly, with the following dedication: 'To a common hero ... walking in countless thousands on the streets' (de Certeau, 1984, p. v).

Today, of course, those who are 'walking in countless thousands on the streets' (ibid.) often do so while carrying mobile media technologies, and this means that it is now necessary to expand on de Certeau's account of moving about on foot. Making direct reference to his social theory, Caroline Bassett (2003, pp. 344–5) contributes to such an expansion in a piece on mobile-phone use:

I still walk in the city. But I am no longer a pedestrian in the old sense because ... the city streets are full of virtual doorways. ... Countless ways through, ways out and ways in to the city ... are constructed by ... mobile-phone ... use. This change ... means that ... I can walk ... in the streets and simultaneously connect with other people ... far away. ... I can be reached on my mobile phone but also ... I can use it to reach out ... to move and act in multiple spaces.

What she seeks to do here, then, is precisely to develop de Certeau's notions of movement, action and space, by putting the matter of getting around in urban physical environments together with the matter of technologically mediated mobility or of finding ways about in media environments. Incidentally, it is worth noting Bassett's choice of the word 'reach', as it also appears, in a rather different context, in the literature of phenomenological geography (Buttimer, 1980; and see Silverstone, 1994, pp. 27–8, for a brief but insightful consideration of Buttimer's concept of reach in relation to television and other media of communication).

Like Bassett, Thrift (2004a, 2007) looks to develop de Certeau's ideas about 'ordinary practitioners of the city' (de Certeau, 1984, p. 93) by taking account of technology. More specifically, he wants to 'take into account the rise of automobility' and explore 'the practice of driving'

(Thrift, 2007, p. 75), which, given the significance of the car as an element of 'our "technological unconscious"' in contemporary urban living, is strangely absent from de Certeau's analysis. Perhaps it is because de Certeau takes 'the practice of walking ... as a sign of the human' (ibid.) that he neglects the practice of driving, regarding this activity, which is itself a sort of technologically mediated mobility, as somehow less embodied and therefore less human than walking. However, in Thrift's view, driving, and 'passengering' too, are 'both profoundly embodied and sensuous experiences' (ibid., p. 80). In fact, one of the key features of his broader theoretical perspective, which I will be outlining shortly, is that humans ought not to be approached 'as separate from the thing world', since the human is a 'tool-being' (ibid., p. 10). For Thrift, then, the boundaries between bodies and technologies are blurred and unclear. In the case of car driving, there is the emergence of a hybrid 'person-thing' (of what Katz, 1999, p. 33, calls a 'humanized car' or an 'automobilized person').

Drawing on research findings reported by sociologist Jack Katz (1999), who, with his students, had carried out an investigation of driving behaviour in the city of Los Angeles, Thrift (2007, p. 81) asserts that 'drivers experience cars as extensions of their bodies' (this notion of technologies as extensions of bodies and the senses clearly echoes the first-generation medium theory of McLuhan, 1994 [1964], outlined in the previous chapter), and he notes that 'as a result of this ... driving can ... be a highly emotional experience' (see also Sheller, 2008 [2004]). In addition, driving practices might usefully be understood, in de Certeau's terms, as creative or tactical in character, as long as this does not lead to an unrealistically romantic view of driving as a form of political resistance. Just as the pedestrian makes 'shortcuts and detours' (de Certeau, 1984, p. 98), so the experienced urban driver is involved in going down 'streets that ... carry little traffic ... using another car as a "screen" in order to merge onto a highway' (Katz, 1999, p. 36) and so on. Similarly, just as walking helps to constitute places, so cars can be, in two linked ways, 'a means of habitation, of dwelling' (Amin and Thrift, 2002, p. 101; and yet it is vital to acknowledge that there may be frictions between the place-making activities of pedestrians and car drivers). First, cars 'inhabit the road', and, second, they 'are a habitation in themselves' (ibid.). In relation to the latter point, cars have the potential to become routinely lived-in, 'homely' locations for drivers, and they now come equipped with 'sound systems ... in-car navigation systems ... climate control ... ergonomically designed interiors ... and the like' (Thrift, 2007, pp. 84–5).

Working in the field of media studies, Michael Bull (2001) has investigated in greater detail how 'sound systems' are employed in cars. He focuses on the 'auditory' aspects of 'automobile habitation' (Bull, 2001, p. 187; see also Bull, 2007, pp. 87–107), and his empirical research material on the car as a 'sound environment' therefore serves as a valuable supplement to Thrift's analysis of 'automobility'. Consider, for example, the following account from one of Bull's research participants:

> When I get in my car and I turn on my radio, I'm at home. I haven't got a journey to make before I get home. I'm already home. ... I wind the window down so I can hear what's going on and sometimes as the sun's setting ... I'm in town and I think ... what a beautiful city ... I'm living in.
>
> (Bull, 2001, p. 185)

There are three brief points that I want to make about this quote. First, the driver's at-homeness in the car is evident here because it is expressed verbally (although, as I noted in my earlier discussion of Tuan's work, such environmental experience is not always translatable into words), and that experience of being-at-home is evidently bound up with the car's sound environment. It is realised by the routine act of switching on the radio. Second, it is necessary to add that the driver's sound environment is by no means limited to what is heard on the radio. When the driver says 'I wind the window down so I can hear what's going on', it is clear that there is a doubling of the audible as the familiar sounds of the radio and the city intermingle. Third, it is also necessary to add that the driver's experience is a multi-sensual one. For instance, as well as hearing the sounds of the radio and the city, there is the sight of the setting sun and the shifting urban visual scene. Then there is the sense of touch involved in switching on the radio, along with the touch and bodily coordination that would obviously be involved in holding and turning the steering wheel, moving the gearstick, operating the various foot pedals and so on.

Non-representational Theory

In this section and the one following it, I offer short commentaries on two approaches in the contemporary social sciences and humanities that are closely related. Indeed, my first commentary will merge into the second. Getting to grips with these approaches is not easy. It requires an engagement with what are sometimes quite difficult concepts and issues, which are likely to be unfamiliar to many students in the field of media studies. Even so, I want to propose that the rewards of engaging with this material outweigh any difficulties encountered in the process, because the approaches in question have the potential to challenge certain established modes of media (and cultural) analysis, and to open up or, putting it more modestly, to widen alternative lines of inquiry.

When Cresswell (2008, p. 55) points to the connections between Tuan's experiential perspective and 'much of the most exciting work' that is going on today, he is thinking, at least partly, about the ways in which the phenomenological geography of the 1970s foreshadowed the emergence of non-representational theory within contemporary human geography in the UK. Non-representational theory is a term that appears consistently in Thrift's writings from the mid-1990s onwards (for example, Thrift, 1996, 1999, 2004b, 2007), and my outline of that approach here will be based chiefly on a consideration of his arguments, developing what I have already written in the previous section about his analysis of automobility. However, it should be remembered that many others, including several academics who were once doctoral students in Thrift's department during the 1990s, are working in the same area (for example, see Anderson and Harrison, 2010a, for a recent collection of essays by geographers on 'non-representational theories'). It should be remembered, too, that, although I am citing non-representational theory as an instance of contemporary work, and while Thrift employs the term as a label for his own writings, he also uses it to name, retrospectively, a tradition of analysis in philosophy and social theory that is both long and broad. Like the phenomenological geographers before him, he is influenced by the philosophy of Martin Heidegger and Maurice Merleau-Ponty, claiming them as non-representational theorists (see the diagram that he presents in Thrift, 1999, p. 303). Further influences include the 'micro-sociology' (Thrift, 2004b, p. 99) of Erving Goffman, Harold Garfinkel and others, which was of interest to Meyrowitz (1985) and Scannell (1996), in addition to the social theory of de Certeau and his compatriot Pierre Bourdieu, whose work will feature at a later stage in the chapter.

Ben Anderson (2009, p. 503), who is part of a younger generation of non-representational theorists in the discipline of geography, helpfully characterises the approach as an attempt to explore 'the taking-place of practices', and he emphasises the point that 'non-representational theories are theories of practice'. This means that they focus primarily on what people, as well as 'non-human ... actants' (ibid., p. 504), are doing. Indeed, when Thrift (1996, p. 1) initially sets out his agenda for non-representational theory, he admits to an academic 'obsession ... with the sensuousness of practice'.

Within the general project of investigating practices or 'doings', the 'main tenets' of non-representational theory include a concern to 'pay more attention to the pre-cognitive' (Thrift, 2007, p. 7) in everyday living, and also a linked concern with 'stressing affect' (ibid., p. 12), as Tuan had started to do years earlier with his assertions about place and attachment (but see Thrift, 1999, p. 319, for a brief, mixed assessment of previous 'phenomenological work on place'). In addition, there is Thrift's overlapping interest in 'the way in which the human body interacts with ... things' (Thrift, 2007, p. 10), on which I have already commented with specific reference to 'cars as extensions of ... bodies' (ibid., p. 81; and see Thrift, 1996, pp. 40–1, who acknowledges the 'extension of bodily capacities made possible through ... various media of telecommunications').

For the purposes of this outline of non-representational theory, let me look in a little more detail at what Thrift has to say about the significance of 'the pre-cognitive' (elsewhere, Thrift, 2004b, p. 85, prefers the word 'non-cognitive'), because that theme has not been addressed explicitly thus far in my chapter and it is one to which I will be returning in due course (for example, with reference to Merleau-Ponty, 2002 [1962]). Thrift (2004b, p. 90) insists that 'only the smallest part of thinking is explicitly cognitive', following up his statement with a question (with an answer and some further explanation, too):

> Where, then, does ... the other thinking lie? It lies in the body. ... It lies in ... all the senses. ... Notice ... that ... none of this is meant to suggest that cognition is not important. Rather, it is ... to radically extend what thinking might be.

That attempt 'to radically extend what thinking might be' involves attending to 'thought-in-action' (Thrift, 1996, p. 7) or, better still, to 'practical knowing' (Thrift, 2007, p. 121) and 'embodied dispositions' (ibid., p. 58) in everyday environments.

Another reason for considering the importance of the pre- or non-cognitive here is that it helps to explain Thrift's selection of the word 'non-representational'. To some extent, his vocabulary choice was bound up with a frustration over the way in which many human geographers in the 1980s and beyond, and particularly those based in the area of cultural geography, had been focusing their attention on the structures of 'symbolic representations' at the expense of attending to 'actions and interactions' (Thrift, 1996, p. 6; and see Wylie, 2007, who discusses, for instance, the notion of 'landscape-as-text' in cultural geography, contrasting it with contemporary 'landscape phenomenologies'). At the same time, though, Thrift writes of the non-representational in a way that links up with philosophical debates about subjectivity and perception. In line with the phenomenological philosophy of Heidegger and Merleau-Ponty, he contests conceptions of human being that are associated with 'rationalism' and 'cognitivism', and which have now filtered into common sense (Thrift, 1996, pp. 9–14; see also Taylor, 2006; Carman, 2008). Putting it as straightforwardly as I can, such conceptions or models have tended to assume a separation of 'inner' subject and 'outer' world (of mind and body too), in which that external world is perceived by means of mental 'representations' (and the body is an object directed by rational thought or 'cognition'). The main problem with these models is that, when starting out with this sort of separation, it is hard to appreciate 'how meanings ... emerge from practices ... in the world' (Anderson and Harrison, 2010b, p. 6). In contrast, 'non-representational models' (Thrift, 1996, p. 6) reject the dualisms of self/world and mind/body, emphasising the 'engaged ... embodied agency' (Taylor, 2006, pp. 210–11) of 'being-in-the-world' (Heidegger, 1962; Dreyfus, 1991).

Philosopher Charles Taylor (2006, p. 212) provides a clear explanation of what such an engaged, embodied agency involves:

> Being this kind of agent means one has an implicit understanding, what Heidegger at one point calls a 'pre-understanding', of what it is to act, to get around in the world, the way we do. But this is not a matter of representations. The rationalist epistemology induces us to jump to this conclusion because it construes all our understanding as made up of representational bits ... this is not at all what pre-understanding is like. ... To know one's way about is to be really moving around, handling things. ... This background sense of reality is nonrepresentational, because it is something we possess in ... our actual dealings with things ... it is a kind of 'knowing how'.

This is exactly what Thrift (2004b, p. 90) is getting at when he argues that there is much thinking which 'lies in the body ... the senses' (indeed, it is possible to go further and argue that all 'thinking', even 'the smallest part' that 'is explicitly cognitive', still has a connection with bodily experiences of the world, since there is no separable, disengaged and disembodied 'mind'). In the course of everyday living within familiar material environments, there is a pre-cognitive understanding or 'bodily understanding' (Carman, 2008, p. 99), which is intimately connected to 'our actual dealings with things' (Taylor, 2006, p. 212). It is a practical knowing, a knowing how 'to act, to get around in the world'. Walking and driving in the city, as well as passing through 'virtual doorways' (Bassett, 2003, p. 345) and 'moving around' in media settings, would serve as good examples of routine activities that incorporate this type of know-how. I will come to more examples soon, including several that literally involve 'handling things'.

The Dwelling Perspective

It is not just in human geography but in social anthropology, too, that phenomenology has been influential (for instance, see Jackson, 1996, for a collection of essays in 'phenomenological anthropology'; see also Howes, 2003; Pink, 2009, on a 'sensual turn' in anthropology, and in contemporary ethnographic research more broadly, which has been inspired at least partly by phenomenological insights). In the present section, I consider some aspects of the work of a social anthropologist called Tim Ingold (2000, 2007, 2008; Lee and Ingold, 2006). I will be focusing here on what he names, making direct reference to Heidegger (1993 [1971]), 'a "dwelling perspective"' (Ingold, 2000, p. 154).

As with Thrift's non-representational theory, Ingold's dwelling perspective rejects the 'rationalist' view of a 'separation between the perceiver and the world', such that the perceiver has to reconstruct the world, in the mind, prior to any meaningful engagement with it' (ibid., p. 178). Ingold (ibid., p. 172) contends that in his own discipline of anthropology a version of this view has been 'fairly conventional', and so, as a consequence, people are often seen to live out their relationships to the world cognitively, through 'a framework of symbolic meanings ... which gives shape to ... experience and direction to ... action' (ibid., p. 160). He cites the example of Clifford Geertz's well-known anthropological work (see especially Geertz, 1973). There, social life is understood as a sort of 'text' and people are thought to be 'suspended' in its 'webs of significance' (ibid., p. 5).

I want to suggest that a similar kind of view can be found in those strands of media studies which have, in one way or another, privileged 'representation' or 'textuality' (my suggestion applies equally to the neighbouring field of cultural studies, although see, for example, Willis, 2000, p. 20, for a critique of 'the language paradigm' in cultural studies and for an accompanying focus on 'the sensuousness of cultural practices, including the sensuous use of objects', which serves to align his approach with non-representational theories). Therefore, I suspect that Ingold, and Thrift too, would have problems with certain aspects of media theory and research, especially where there has been a longstanding concern with the structural analysis of 'media representations' (what used to be called 'message content', see Meyrowitz, 1985), and even where the emphasis has been on investigating people's cognitive interpretations of these representations or 'texts', including technologies-as-texts (some of my own early writings can be seen to have that emphasis, most notably Moores, 1993a). Having made that point, though, I should add that Thrift (1996, p. 8) does not seek to deny 'the reality of representations'. Instead, non-representational theorists approach language and symbolic representation 'as performative ... as doings' (rather than, say, simply 'as ... ideologies ... as a code', see Dewsbury et al., 2002, p. 438). Pursuing this line of argument, it is my contention that media uses are best approached as doings or as embodied practices (see also Couldry, 2010, pp. 37–40, on 'practice as an emerging theme in media research'). This is because there is more to media use than 'encodings' or 'decodings' (see Hall, 1980; Morley, 1980, for founding statements of this kind of social semiotics in media studies), and considerably more than psychological 'gratifications' (Blumler and Katz, 1974).

From the dwelling perspective, as in non-representational theory, there is an emphasis on what Ingold (2000, p. 173) calls 'the agent-in-its-environment', or being-in-the-world, and on what Thrift (1999, p. 308) calls 'the primacy of practices'. Drawing on phenomenological philosophy (as well as on the 'ecological approach' of Gibson, 1986 [1979]), Ingold (2000, p. 153) associates dwelling with 'immersion ... in an environment or lifeworld'. However, in associating dwelling with 'immersion', he is quite clear that there is 'more to dwelling than the mere fact of occupation' (ibid., p. 185). For him, then, 'it is through being inhabited ... that the world becomes ... meaningful ... for people', as they 'make themselves at home in the world' (ibid., pp. 172–3) through their routine practices. As he explains in more detail:

> Meanings are not attached by the mind to objects in the world ... rather these objects take on their significance ... by virtue of their incorporation into a ... pattern of day-to-day activities. In short ...

meaning is ... in the relational contexts of people's practical engagement with their lived-in environments.

(ibid., p. 168)

Challenging further rationalism's assumed 'separation between the perceiver and the world', he continues: 'self and world merge in the activity of dwelling, so that one cannot say where one ends and the other begins' (ibid., p. 169).

In Ingold's book, *The Perception of the Environment: Essays in Livelihood, Dwelling and Skill*, he proceeds to discuss his dwelling perspective in relation to the skills of wayfinding. Dealing with this particular aspect of his approach will take me back, once again, to a theme of Tuan's (Tuan, 1977). It will also enable me to make a link forward, though, with Ingold's more recent work on place and movement, which includes his involvement in collaborative ethnographic research (for instance, see Lee and Ingold, 2006).

Consider what Ingold (2000, p. 219) has to say in the following lengthy extract (his main purpose here is to provide a critique of the psychological concept of 'cognitive maps'):

Everyone has probably had the experience, at some time or other, of feeling lost, or of not knowing in which way to turn in order to reach a desired destination. Yet for most of the time we know where we are, and how to get to where we want to go. Ordinary life would be well-nigh impossible if we did not. It remains a challenge, however, to account for everyday skills of orientation and wayfinding. ... For the map-using stranger ... in unfamiliar country, 'being here' or 'going there' generally entails the ability to identify one's current or intended future position with a certain spatial ... location, defined by the intersection of particular coordinates on the map. But a person who has grown up in a country ... knows quite well ... in what direction to go, without having to consult an artefactual map. ... According to a view that has found wide support ... there is no difference in principle between them. Both are map-users. ... The difference is just that the native inhabitant's map is held ... in the head, preserved not on paper but in memory, in the form of a comprehensive spatial representation ... or 'cognitive' map. ... I ... argue, to the contrary, that there is no such map.

In marked opposition to this idea of the ' "cognitive" map', he explains 'what it means to know one's whereabouts' (ibid.) via the concept of 'ambulatory knowing', which points to how 'people's knowledge of the environment' is formed 'in the very course of their moving about in it' (ibid., p. 230). 'I would prefer to say', writes Ingold (ibid., p. 229), 'that we know as we go.' It is not that people carry with them in their minds a mental representation of space that they access to guide their bodily movements, but rather that their knowledge and experience is, to borrow Thrift's phrase from a different context, 'profoundly embodied and sensuous' (Thrift, 2007, p. 80). In other words, this knowledge of the environment is pre-cognitive or non-representational. As Ingold (2007, p. 89) puts it a few years later, 'the ways of knowing of inhabitants go along ... inhabitant knowledge ... is alongly integrated'.

Like de Certeau (1984), Ingold is interested in walking practices, although not just in urban settings. With fellow anthropologist Jo Lee, he has been involved in an ethnographic research project on walking in northeastern Scotland (in rural areas as well as in the city of Aberdeen; see also Gray, 2003 [1999], for a report of earlier anthropological field-work on the walking and motorbiking practices of sheep farmers who made themselves at home in the hills of the Scottish Borders). With an eye to Ingold's previous criticism of Geertz (1973), the 'phenomenolog-ically inspired fieldwork' (Lee and Ingold, 2006, p. 83) that they carried out led them to argue that ' "webs of significance" ... are comprised of trails that are trodden on the ground, not spun in the symbolic ether, as people make their way about'. Furthermore, Lee and Ingold (ibid., p. 76) argue that: 'Places ... are actually constituted by ... movements to, from and around.' With regard to 'movements ... around', they refer to the fact that: 'There are many examples in our research of ... oft-repeated walks ... and circuits ... that ... in their repetition ... might be seen as "thick lines" of ... meaningful place-making' (ibid., pp. 77–8; and note that it is possible to hear echoes of Tuan, 1977, p. 182, who reflected on how, through habitual use, 'the path ... acquires a density of meaning', so that the path 'and the pauses along it constitute a ... place'). Meanwhile, with regard to movements 'to' and 'from', Ingold (2007, p. 2) has posed the vital question: 'how could there be places ... if people did not come and go?'

Ingold's emphasis on defining place in relation to 'trails' or 'lines' of movement has recently caused him to 'somewhat regret' his centring of 'the concept of dwelling', which can have, in his words, 'a heavy conno-tation of snug, well-wrapped localism' (Ingold, 2008, p. 1808). 'The concept of habitation is not so loaded', concludes Ingold (ibid.). Such a 'snug, well-wrapped localism' may occasionally be found in discussions of dwelling. For instance, it is undoubtedly there for me when I read

Heidegger's nostalgic account of 'a farmhouse in the Black Forest ... on the wind-sheltered mountain slope ... among the meadows close to the spring' (Heidegger, 1993 [1971], pp. 361–2). Perhaps it is also there, to a lesser degree, in Tuan's reference to 'a favorite armchair' (Tuan, 1977, p. 149), which I cited earlier in the chapter, because his example evokes for me a cosy, enclosed scene of fireside warmth. However, I do not believe that identifying particular instances like these in the phenomenological literature requires the concept of dwelling to be dropped. Rather, matters of dwelling or habitation always need to be theorised in relation to mobility of different sorts at different levels. There are the localised movements 'around' that Lee and Ingold (2006) report on, but they also acknowledge that place is constituted, in part, by the comings-and-goings in and out of locations. Of course, such comings-and-goings are not only on foot, as they are often technologically mediated in various ways (on this important theme, Massey, 1994, pp. 146–56, writes helpfully of 'a global sense of place' in contemporary living, and her ideas are to be considered at length in the following chapter of my book; see also Tuan, 1996b, p. 183, on 'the concept of "cosmopolitan hearth"').

Practical Engagement with Lived-in Environments

At what is roughly the halfway point in a lengthy chapter, let me briefly summarise the material that I have covered so far. With the aim of extending my discussion of media and situational geography from the previous chapter, I began this one by turning to Tuan's phenomenological geography (especially Tuan, 1977, 2004) for a definition of place as an experiential accomplishment that binds people and environments (including media environments). I then went on to link Tuan's pioneering work on place-constituting activities with de Certeau's pragmatics of everyday living, Thrift's non-representational theory and Ingold's dwelling perspective. The common thread running through these approaches is a concern with how 'meaning is ... in the relational contexts of people's practical engagement with their lived-in environments' (Ingold, 2000, p. 168). Both in Ingold's arguments for a dwelling perspective within social anthropology and in the closely related area of non-representational theory within contemporary human geography, such a concern is compared favourably with views that are focused on the cognitive and representational dimensions of social life. As Thrift (2004b, p. 90) concedes, it would clearly be a mistake 'to suggest that cognition is not important' (or to deny the reality of representations, see Thrift, 1996, p. 8), yet any investigation of the sensuousness of practices or doings involves attending to pre-cognitive or bodily understandings of everyday environments: 'the myriad ways subjects inhabit the world before they represent that world to themselves and others' (Anderson and Harrison, 2010b, p. 10).

All of this has serious implications for considering the ways in which media studies are (and might be) carried out. It raises questions about the limitations of those forms of media analysis that have been focused rather too tightly on the symbolic and the interpretative. It calls for an appreciation of media uses as place-constituting activities, among a range of other such activities in everyday living. It calls for a linked appreciation of the environmental experiences of media users, and their 'inhabitant knowledge' (Ingold, 2007, p. 89) of physical and media environments, which is, in Ingold's terms, 'alongly integrated'. It also calls for an appreciation of everyday practices, including routine practices of media use, as embodied. As Tony Bennett (2005, p. 93) indicates, most previous approaches to the relationships between media and their users have tended to be concerned with 'the content of media messages ... and ... with audience ... interpretation', and while there is 'no discounting the importance of these concerns ... they do suggest a view of audiences as essentially disembodied, as if ... relations to the media take place without ... eyes, ears ... and fingers being particularly involved' (for a similar assessment in the field of literary studies, see Littau, 2006, p. 10, who contends that 'the reader' is too often theorised there as 'a disembodied mind rather than a physiological being sitting at the edge of his or her seat, tears welling up ... spine tingling').

In the next section, my emphasis is precisely on issues of embodiment. Bodies have been important for most of the academic authors cited in the present chapter, but I turn now to Merleau-Ponty's phenomenological philosophy and especially to his *Phenomenology of Perception* (2002 [1962]), which was a key reference point for later work on embodied practices. Whereas Ingold (2004), via his interest in practices of walking, writes of 'the world perceived through the feet', I want to concentrate on what Merleau-Ponty (2002 [1962], p. 166), in his account of the acquisition of habit, calls 'knowledge in the hands'.

Knowledge in the Hands

Contemporary philosopher Taylor Carman (2008, p. 19) explains that, for Merleau-Ponty: 'Perception is not mental representation ... but skillful bodily orientation ... in given circumstances.' Indeed, in a short explanatory commentary on his own work, Merleau-Ponty (2004 [1964], pp. 34–7) confirms that he has sought 'to re-establish the roots of the mind in its body and in its world', writing of an 'incarnate subject':

> In my ... *Phenomenology of Perception* ... the body is no longer merely an object in the world, under the purview of a separated spirit. It is on the side of the subject ... it inhabits ... space. It applies itself to space like a hand to an instrument. ... We grasp ... space through our bodily situation. A 'corporeal ... schema' gives us ... a ... practical ... notion of the relation between ... body and things, of our hold on them.

What I find particularly interesting in this passage, along with Merleau-Ponty's critique of the mind/body dualism (he insists that one's body is not simply 'an object for an "I think"', see Merleau-Ponty, 2002 [1962], p. 177; also Romdenh-Romluc, 2011, p. 62, on Merleau-Ponty and 'bodily subjectivity'), is his use of the terms 'grasp' and 'hold', and his reference to the way in which bodies inhabit space by applying themselves to it 'like a hand to an instrument'. In this case, the terms are being employed metaphorically in order to make a general point about the incarnate subject and what he names its 'corporeal schema', but elsewhere, in a fascinating section of *Phenomenology of Perception* (Merleau-Ponty, 2002 [1962]), pp. 164–70), he supplies some specific examples of 'the relation between ... body and things' (things that are 'ready-to-hand', see Heidegger, 1962, pp. 98–9, on the hammer as a tool), which include more literal references to the habitual and skilful movements of human hands.

Perhaps the best known of Merleau-Ponty's examples there is that of the 'blind man's stick' (Merleau-Ponty, 2002 [1962], p. 165). Once a person gets 'used to' the stick and has it 'well in hand' (ibid., pp. 165–6), its point 'has become an area of sensitivity, extending the scope and active radius of touch, and providing a parallel to sight'. Merleau-Ponty (ibid., pp. 175–6) goes on to say later that 'the stick has become a familiar instrument ... a bodily auxiliary ... the world of feelable things ... now begins ... not at the outer skin of the hand, but at the end of the stick'. Through habitual and skilful manipulation, such sticks may become extensions of bodies and the senses, as they are 'incorporated' by their users and consequently recede or 'withdraw' as objects (see Ihde, 1990, pp. 31–41, who cites Merleau-Ponty's example of the stick, as well as Heidegger's example of the hammer, in opening up a discussion of technology and embodiment relations). A further example that Merleau-Ponty offers is that of a musical instrument, the organ (see also Sudnow, 1993 [1979], on learning to play the piano). In discussing the practices of an experienced player, he makes a valuable point about the transposable character of the bodily habits and skills that are involved. Learning to play the organ (an activity that does typically require formal instruction) is about gradually developing a durable set of embodied dispositions, but it is important to note that there is the development, too, of a degree of flexibility and adaptability. It is not just a matter of fixed movements that are learnt in order to be repeated over and over in a mechanistic fashion. Merleau-Ponty's account of the acquisition of habit is more subtle than this. He observes how a highly experienced organist is still able to play proficiently on an organ with a layout that is not exactly the same as the instrument with which that player is familiar. During the rehearsal period, then, the organist 'incorporates ... the relevant directions and dimensions, settles into the organ as one settles into a house' (Merleau-Ponty, 2002 [1962], p. 168). What is evident in such cases is a particular sensual and emotional 'feel' for playing, which, after a while spent at the keyboard, allows the organist to be at home with the slightly different layout of the new instrument and, as a result, to become immersed in the sounds of the music. As Ingold (2000, p. 414) puts it in a related discussion of skilled musical performance, 'the boundaries between the player, the instrument and the acoustic environment appear to dissolve'.

The last example of Merleau-Ponty's that I want to deal with here is one involving other kinds of key, namely those situated on a typewriter (it is worth noting that when the original French edition of *Phenomenology of Perception* was published in the mid-1940s, the typewriter was not the old, outmoded technology it is today). He states that:

> It is possible to know how to type without being able to say where the letters which make the words are to be found on the banks of keys. ... The subject knows where the letters are on the typewriter as we know where one of our limbs is, through a knowledge bred of familiarity. ... It is knowledge in the hands, which is forthcoming ... when bodily effort is made.
>
> (Merleau-Ponty, 2002 [1962], p. 166)

His crucial point about the knowledge in the hands of the skilled typist, which is a 'knowledge bred of familiarity', is broadened out when he asserts that 'it is the body which "understands" in the acquisition of habit' (ibid., p. 167). Merleau-Ponty (ibid.) is well aware that, from a rationalist viewpoint, this 'way of putting it will appear absurd', and yet, he argues, 'the phenomenon of habit is just what prompts us to revise our notion of "understand" and our notion of the body'. The acquisition of habit has to do with 'a rearrangement ... of the corporeal schema' (ibid., p. 164), which is bound up with the constitution of 'our precognitive familiarity with ... the world' (Carman, 2008, p. 106). In the case of typewriter use, 'the banks of keys' come to feel thoroughly familiar over time, and 'the subject who learns to type incorporates the key-bank space into ... bodily space' (Merleau-Ponty, 2002 [1962], p. 167).

An updated example is proffered by sociologist Nick Crossley (2001, p. 122), who, drawing on Merleau-Ponty's phenomenological approach, writes in some detail about his own experience of using a computer keyboard:

> I can type and to that extent 'I know' where the various letters are on the keyboard. I do not have to find the letters one by one. ... My fingers just move in the direction of the correct keys ... however ... I could not give a reflective, discursive account of the keyboard layout. I do not 'know' where the keys are in a reflective sense and to make any half-decent attempt at guessing I have to imagine that I am typing and watch where my fingers head for. ... The type of knowledge I have of the keyboard is a practical, embodied knowledge ... distinct from discursive knowledge.

What Crossley (ibid., pp. 122–3) tries to get at in his description is an 'embodied form of "knowing without knowing"' or 'bodily know-how', which he has real difficulty in accessing if he is away from the technology and not actually engaged in the activity. Indeed, in such circumstances, 'any half-decent attempt at guessing ... where the keys are' requires that 'bodily effort is made' (Merleau-Ponty, 2002 [1962], p. 166). It is interesting that he employs the term 'pre-reflective' where others tend to refer to the pre-cognitive, as a way of distinguishing his 'knowing without knowing' from the sort of reflective or 'discursive knowledge' that is more conventionally considered to be knowledge: 'I have a pre-reflective ... grasp on my environment, relative to my body, as is evidenced by my capacity to move around in and utilise that space without first having to think how to do so' (Crossley, 2001, p. 122). Of course, that 'capacity to move around ... without first having to think', at least 'in a reflective sense', is not only evident when the fingers move around a keyboard. As suggested at various stages in this chapter, it is a quite fundamental feature of dwelling or habitation.

Before returning to wider matters of dwelling, though, I want to stay a while longer with that particular element of the pre-reflective grasp on everyday environments that Merleau-Ponty calls knowledge in the hands. In my view, one of the most significant contributions to media analysis (and to social theories of mobility) over recent years is John Tomlinson's book, *The Culture of Speed: The Coming of Immediacy* (2007). I value his book because, rather like sociologist John Urry (2000, 2007), whose work on 'mobilities' will be discussed in the following chapter, Tomlinson (2007) combines an interest in the applications of media and communications technology, which he associates with 'the coming of immediacy', with an interest in the historical development of transport technologies and other kinds of 'machine speed'. He therefore looks to understand what he names 'the telemediatization of culture' (ibid., p. 94) partly in relation to experiences of physical travel, which I regard as a welcome move for non-media-centric media studies (see also Morley, 2009, p. 116, who argues for an analysis of 'the articulation of ... communications and physical transport'; and for an extension of his argument, see Morley, forthcoming). At this point in my book, in the context of my notes on Merleau-Ponty, embodied practices and body–thing relations, there is a specific section of *The Culture of Speed* that can helpfully be highlighted (Tomlinson, 2007, pp. 107–11). It is a short section (Tomlinson actually refers to it as 'a slight digression' or 'an excursus') on 'keyboards'.

Tomlinson (ibid., p. 108) announces that he wants 'to draw attention to ... our habitual way of accessing and communicating via keyboards and keypads, practices which do obviously involve the body, particularly the hands and the sense of touch'. Although these practices have 'generally been ignored' (ibid.) in the field of media studies, they deserve attention because:

> Keyboards – or ... the scaled down version, keypads – now saturate our environment. Increasingly, we must use them not just in ... interactions with media and communications systems – on mobile phones, TV ... remote controls, computers, games consoles – but also to draw money from our banks, to cook food in microwave ovens, to open doors, to activate air conditioning, to ... wash ... our cars, to access commentaries in art galleries and museums and so on.

Using keyboards and keypads in these various circumstances of every-day living requires a set of 'acquired habits and sensory-bodily rhythms' (ibid., p. 109). For instance, Tomlinson (ibid., p. 108) comments (from the outsider perspective of a middle-aged academic!) on what he sees as 'the remarkable dexterities that young people seem to possess in text messaging'. This sort of dexterity, 'bred of familiarity' with the keys on a mobile phone, might perhaps be called knowledge in the thumbs (and see Richardson, 2008, for empirical research findings on the 'bodily incorporation' of mobile phones). Tomlinson (2007, p. 108) considers, too, the rhythmic patterns of physical movement involved in remembering those 'codes we have to use ... but must not write down', suggesting that there is 'an embodied form of memory' at work. Interestingly, with regard to Merleau-Ponty's example of typewriter use, he also goes on to compare 'the typical deftness of manipulations of keypads' with the more 'muscular, energetic operations performed on mechanical objects', proposing that 'modern computer keyboards have only the faintest family resemblance to typewriters' (ibid., pp. 109–10).

Running with Tomlinson's point about the importance of 'acquired habits' of the hand in the uses of electronic media and other technologies today, it is possible to identify a further, typically taken-for-granted manual activity that is associated with the 'modern computer'. Mark Nunes (2006, p. 41), with reference to what he terms 'the operational disposition' of a computer user, draws attention to the seemingly unremarkable matter of 'knowing the proper speed to "double click" a mouse'. Indeed, he sees this practical, embodied knowledge as part of a broader range of routine 'point-and-click' (ibid., p. 39) competences, involving the deft manoeuvring of a mouse device, which usually sits on a mat beside the keyboard, while simultaneously finding ways about in the online environments that are displayed on screen.

Nunes's observations on the human–computer 'interface' are particularly helpful for my purposes, since they serve to support the more general argument that I am making for a joint consideration of physical and media environments as lived spaces. In the case of computers (but also in the case of the point-and-press television 'remote controls' that Tomlinson, 2007, p. 108, mentions in passing), the knowledge in the hands of users is intimately caught up with technologically mediated mobility or travel, and these interconnected movements can constitute places. For example, both the familiar material environments of the desks on which home computers are located and the familiar spaces of internet 'home pages', or else the familiar settings of 'spine-tingling' video games, accessed and navigated by way of pointing and clicking, or pressing the buttons on a console, would be places according to Tuan's definition of place as an experiential accomplishment. In addition, this direct link between bodily know-how and technologically mediated mobility leads me to doubt any grand claims about the disembodied character of online existence, and to insist that issues of embodiment should be much more central to media theory and research than they currently are (see also Dreyfus, 2001; Ihde, 2002; Hansen, 2006, for three related but rather different phenomenological takes on bodies, technologies and electronic media of communication).

Everyday Environmental Experience

As I noted near the beginning of this chapter, Tuan (1977, p. v) employs the term 'environmental experience' in dealing with matters of dwelling or habitation, but it is to David Seamon's book, *A Geography of the Lifeworld: Movement, Rest, and Encounter* (1979), that I come now for further consideration of such experience. Although he is many years younger than Tuan, Seamon was a fellow pioneer of phenomenological geography back in the 1970s, when he was doing his postgraduate research (encouraged and overseen by Anne Buttimer), which focused on the topic of 'everyday environmental experience' (ibid., p. 15). Crucially, as well as drawing on the philosophical writings of Heidegger, Bachelard and especially Merleau-Ponty, Seamon's project had a strong empirical element. In the American city where he was studying, he set up a number of what he called 'environmental experience groups' (see ibid., pp. 21–8, for his justification of the 'process of group inquiry ... in which people can come to moments of discovery' through shared exploration, and for lists of the group participants and the themes that they discussed, such as 'the significance of habit and routine', 'everyday movement patterns' and 'emotions relating to place'). Discussions recorded in those groups provided a basis for the analysis set out in Seamon's book, which he characterises as a study of 'people's experiential involvement with their everyday geographical world' (ibid., p. 17).

I will be referring shortly to some examples of the interesting empirical data that emerged from Seamon's research project, but before that I want to do two things. First, I think it is important to emphasise the ground-breaking nature of his work in *A Geography of the Lifeworld* (although I should add that, later in the chapter, I will also be critical of specific aspects of the approach). Second, I want to point to a few of the key terms in his conceptual vocabulary, which feature alongside the concept of everyday environmental experience and which I regard as helpful for investigations of media, place and mobility.

Long before Ingold (2000) advocated a dwelling perspective in social anthropology and developed his critique of the notion of cognitive maps, Seamon (1979, pp. 33–5) had already been highly critical of 'cognitive ... theories of movement', in which 'the cognitive map is a key unit of spatial behavior': 'I argue that cognition plays only a partial role in everyday spatial behavior; that a sizeable portion of our everyday movements at all varieties of environmental scale is pre-cognitive and involves a prereflective knowledge of the body' (compare this with Thrift's assertion, quoted earlier, that 'only the smallest part of thinking is explicitly cognitive ... the other thinking ... lies in the body', see Thrift, 2004b, p. 90). In addition, long before Lee and Ingold (2006) carried out their phenomenologically inspired fieldwork on practices of walking and formations of place, Seamon had already provided valuable empirical findings on the significance of 'everyday movements', including walking and driving, for place-making. Most importantly, though, within the discipline of geography, it must be admitted that Seamon was ahead of non-representational theory in drawing attention to the pre-cognitive, practical knowing and embodied dispositions. However, Thrift's main writings on non-representational theories (notably Thrift, 1996, 1999, 2004b, 2007) contain no references to Seamon, and when other non-representational geographers cite *A Geography of the Lifeworld*, it tends to be discussed only briefly, in passing, as an instance of an outmoded 'humanist' perspective (for example, see Wylie, 2007, p. 180; Anderson and Harrison, 2010b, p. 9). I would therefore suggest that the time is ripe for a re-evaluation of Seamon's work, as Cresswell (2006, p. 31) acknowledges when he states that Seamon's book, particularly with its insights into 'bodily mobility', 'was an important precursor to ... nonrepresentational theory'.

One of the main concepts employed by Seamon (1979, p. 41) in his analysis of 'lifeworld' involvements is that of 'body-subject' (see also Seamon, 1980; he is, of course, building on Merleau-Ponty's argument that 'the body ... is on the side of the subject', Merleau-Ponty, 2004 [1964], pp. 35–6). In referring to the notion of body-subject, Seamon (1979, p. 40) is interested in the 'habitual nature of movement' (that is, in movements that 'occur without or before any conscious intervention'). He proceeds to discuss the ways in which these habitual, everyday movements are integrated into wider 'time-space routines'

(Seamon, 1979, p. 54; there are connections here with Hägerstrand's 'time-geography', see especially Pred, 1996 [1977], and it is worth noting that Hägerstrand wrote the 'foreword' to Buttimer and Seamon, 1980). As a twin concept to body-subject, Seamon (1979, p. 76) also employs the term 'feeling-subject', in his attempt to explain the emotional or affective aspects of contact with environments, and he asserts that 'forces of body and emotion ... intertwined' can give rise to a condition of at-homeness: 'the usually unnoticed, taken-for-granted situation of being comfortable in and familiar with the everyday world in which one lives' (ibid., pp. 70–1).

This vocabulary of body-subject, time-space routines, feeling-subject and at-homeness is designed to deal precisely with issues of habit, affect and attachment to environment in everyday living. There is another key term for Seamon, though, and it is an important one because it points to the public, collaborative dimension of place-constituting activities. He writes of 'place choreographies' or 'place ballets' (ibid., pp. 54–6; see also Seamon, 1980), defining them as 'an interaction of many time-space routines': 'The place ballet can occur in ... streets, neighbourhoods, market places, transportation depots, cafes.' According to Seamon (1979, p. 56), then, these creative, intricate and interactive 'dances' consist of rhythmic patterns of 'continual human activity' in a range of social settings, and they have the potential to foster 'a strong ... sense of place'. Once again, this is an idea of Seamon's that is clearly echoed in the recent work of Thrift (2009, p. 92), who describes the body 'as a link in a larger spatial dance with other ... bodies and things', and notes that place is bound up with 'the way that people, through following daily rhythms of being, just continue to expect the world to keep on turning up' (although his reference there is to the more fashionable 'rhythmanalysis' of Lefebvre, 2004, rather than to Seamon's ground-breaking book).

In the data that Seamon presents in *A Geography of the Lifeworld*, there are numerous illustrative examples of how 'forces of body and emotion' serve to facilitate at-homeness (and not only in the private space of 'the home'), including several that emphasise time-space routines and place choreographies. For instance, he offers the following detailed account of the 'morning routine' of an environmental-experience-group participant:

> Waking at 7.30, making the bed, bathing, dressing, walking out of the house at eight – so one group member described a morning routine that he followed every day but Sunday. From home he

walked to a nearby cafe, picked up a newspaper (which had to be the *New York Times*), ordered his usual fare (one scrambled egg and coffee), and stayed there until nine when he walked to his office. ... 'I like this routine and I've noticed how I'm bothered a bit when a part of it is upset – if the *Times* is sold out, or if the booths are taken and I have to sit at a counter.'

(Seamon, 1979, pp. 55–6)

What Seamon describes in this passage, which includes a direct quote from a recorded group discussion, is a regular 'round' of activities that involved the group member in bodily mobility, both within and between thoroughly familiar spaces. Those practices were habitual, everyday movements of repetition and return (see Tuan, 1977), and as the group member went on to conclude: 'It's not that I figure out this schedule each day – it simply unfolds' (Seamon, 1979, p. 171). In other words, he just continued 'to expect the world to keep on turning up' (Thrift, 2009, p. 92).

The same participant spoke of the 'atmosphere' of the cafe that he frequented each working-day morning 'between eight o'clock and nine':

Several 'regulars' come in during that period ... the telephone repair-man and several elderly people, including one woman named Claire, whom I know and say 'Good morning' to each day. ... Many of these people know each other. The owner ... knows every one of the regulars and what they will usually order. The situation of ... recognising faces ... somehow makes the place warmer.

(Seamon, 1979, p. 171)

This was a particular, local instance of what Seamon terms 'place ballet'. As with de Certeau's pragmatics of everyday living (de Certeau, 1984), there is a danger that the ordinary activities here are being seen in an overly romanticised light. In Seamon's case, of course, there is no suggestion that the activities in question were practices of political resistance, but his dance metaphor does nevertheless imply a rather romantic view of 'life as art' (see Willis, 2000). Still, the participant's words give an indication of the sort of affective attachments that may be formed as 'many time-space routines' (Seamon, 1979, p. 56) are meshed together on a regular basis. The social relations of the cafe environment appear to have been relations of acquaintanceship rather than of close friendship, yet the again-and-again character of the interactions, and, consequently, the 'situation of … recognising faces', served to create a mood of warmth.

There are two further points that I want to make at this stage about Seamon's example of the cafe, although it is an example that I will be referring to once more in the following section of my chapter. First, what helped this group member, and fellow participants in the environmental-experience groups, to reflect on ordered patterns of movement were those rare occasions when part of routine was disrupted. So when 'basic contact' with familiar, taken-for-granted everyday environments got disturbed, even in seemingly minor ways, it gave rise to a 'noticing' of what is typically unnoticed: 'A change in the world as known brings itself to attention' (ibid., p. 117). Such changes were experienced by the cafe-goer in the example as a source of mild irritation, of feeling 'bothered a bit'. Second, from my perspective, it is important to note that one of the mild irritations mentioned by the participant had to do with the occasional absence of a familiar media environment, when the daily paper he was used to had 'sold out' (ibid., p. 56). Reading that paper (much like making the bed, walking out of the house or drinking coffee) was an utterly normal feature of his morning routine, and an integral part of his experiential involvement with an everyday geographical world. Here, I am reminded of Hermann Bausinger's observation that the newspaper can have a ritual function as 'a mark of confirmation' (Bausinger, 1984, p. 344), and so 'reading it proves that the breakfast-time world is still in order' (see also Peterson, 2010, on the daily paper and habit). Indeed, Bausinger (1984) comments on how regular readers experience disruption when, for one reason or another, the paper that they usually regard 'as "no big deal"' (Scannell, 1996, p. 177) is unavailable.

While Seamon's data contain surprisingly few references to media use, given the location of his study in a US city, scattered fragments of his empirical research material point to media as elements of a lifeworld (and see Seamon, 2006). For instance, in the context of an early-evening routine, the brother of one of the group members is reported to have regularly eaten his meal 'in front of the seven o'clock news on television' (Seamon, 1979, p. 56). Elsewhere, someone reported on the ritual of reading a book in a favourite chair before going to bed each night (see ibid., p. 178). A rather different example involves the telephone: 'A few times when using the phone, I've found myself dialling my home number rather than the one I want … I guess because that number is the one I call the most often' (ibid., pp. 164–5). The connection with my earlier discussion of Merleau-Ponty, the acquisition of habit and knowledge in the hands is clear in this last example.

Hanging Out in the Virtual Pub

Now compare Seamon's example of the cafe and its place ballet (ibid., p. 171) with the following ethnographic description:

> The Falcon is a small, out-of-the-way place, known mainly to its regulars. ... As usual around lunchtime, the bar is crowded. A few people sit singly at tables, but most sit in small groups, often milling around from table to table to chat with others. As in many such local bars and pubs, most of the regulars here are male. Many of them work for a handful of computer companies in a nearby high-tech industry enclave. The atmosphere is loud, casual, and clubby, even raucous. Everybody knows each other.
>
> (Kendall, 2002, pp. 1–2)

As the author of the account goes on to explain, 'The Falcon' was not to be found 'in a back street in Berkeley' (ibid., p. 3), because this is a description of 'a hangout on an online forum'. In fact, it is a passage from near the start of a book that I cited towards the end of the previous chapter, Lori Kendall's *Hanging Out in the Virtual Pub: Masculinities and Relationships Online*. The virtual pub that she writes about, much like the cafe discussed by Seamon's group member, had its own mood of warmth, at least for those who were familiar with its layout and comfortable with the social conventions of its 'chat'. It was a public space inhabited by several 'regulars' who were recognisable to each other, many of whose time-space routines were meshed together (hence their shared 'lunchtime' period on 'Pacific standard time', see ibid., p. 23). Its atmosphere was louder and the social positions of its customers were rather different, but there seems to be, once more, a creative dance of human activity and a collaborative process of place-making. Kendall (ibid., p. 6) argues, then, that such a 'synchronous' media setting, which allows for 'near-instantaneous response ... can provide a particularly vivid sense of "place" ... of gathering together with other people'.

Of course, the idea of a 'virtual place' is not exclusive to Kendall's work. Other internet researchers had the idea well before her. For instance, William Mitchell (1995, p. 22), who is both an architectural and a media theorist, writes of 'virtual places' that 'serve as shared access, multiuser locations' (and outside academia, too, spatial metaphors such as 'site' and 'room' feature widely in ordinary talk about internet communications). The revealing word in the quote from Mitchell, though, is 'locations', because, like Meyrowitz and Scannell, he conceptualises place primarily as a location, rather than as a practical and emotional accomplishment. To some extent, Kendall's work has the same definitional limitations, since she tends to use the term 'place' interchangeably with 'space'. However, she moves a little closer to Tuan and Seamon in her understanding of place when she stresses the routinely lived-in quality of the 'pub' that figures in her ethnography, along with the emotional or affective aspects of action and interaction in this online environment.

I have chosen to put Kendall's example of the virtual pub alongside Seamon's example of the cafe because it helps to strengthen my case that there can be at-homeness in a media setting as well as in a physical setting, but this is not my only reason for returning to Kendall's book at this stage. I want not just to note the similarities between their examples, but also to highlight a distinguishing characteristic of Kendall's perspective on what Seamon calls at-homeness. As a critical sociologist, Kendall has important things to say about social difference and power, which need to be taken on board when thinking about place-constituting activities.

In *Hanging Out in the Virtual Pub*, Kendall (2002) has an interest in the ongoing performance of gendered identities and relationships. She comments at the outset on how 'most of the regulars … are male' (ibid., p. 2) and her concern with gender is mainly one with how certain sorts of masculinity are 'done', both online and offline. This doing involved specific forms of sociable talk-in-interaction: 'Patterns of speech, persistent topics, and a particular style of references to women' (ibid., p. 72). As noted in my previous chapter, the topics of 'insider' conversation in the virtual pub often revolved around technical issues to do with computing, and more generally, as Kendall (ibid., p. 100) puts it, the atmosphere in that bar 'casts women as outsiders unless and until they prove themselves able to perform masculinities'. As a female researcher entering into this 'gendered environment', she found that she had 'to become one of the boys' (ibid., p. 98) in order to maintain access. This suggests to me a broader point. While places are indeed constituted in part by comings and goings, 'geographies of exclusion' (Sibley, 1995) still have to be addressed.

To Sociologise Phenomenological Analysis

Up to now, apart from a few minor quibbles, my take on the phenomenological perspectives reviewed in this chapter has been a positive one.

I am highly sympathetic to these perspectives because of what they can offer to the study of media uses, and, more broadly, because of their valuable insights into the incarnate subject, the acquisition of habit and the agent-in-its-environment. However, the last three sections of the chapter, beginning with the present one, will be rather more critical in tone. In the penultimate and concluding sections that are to follow, I will be concerned, once again, to contest claims about increasing place-lessness in contemporary society, looking first at Edward Relph's phenomenological geography of *Place and Placelessness* (2008 [1976]) and then at Marc Augé's later anthropology of *Non-places* (2009 [1995]). For now, though, leading on from Kendall's points about social difference and power (Kendall, 2002), I want to look at Bourdieu's contention that it is vital 'to sociologize ... phenomenological analysis' (Bourdieu and Wacquant, 1992, p. 73; and remember here that Bourdieu is among those social theorists identified by Thrift, 1999, p. 303, as an influence on his non-representational theory).

Interestingly, one of Bourdieu's academic collaborators, Loïc Wacquant (Bourdieu and Wacquant, 1992, p. 20), describes him as Merleau-Ponty's 'sociological heir', remarking that Bourdieu 'builds in particular on ... Merleau-Ponty's idea of the intrinsic corporeality of ... contact between subject and world'. Bourdieu's social theory, according to Wacquant (ibid., p. 19), 'seeks to capture ... the knowledge without cognitive intent ... that agents acquire of their social world by way of ... immersion within it'. The links with Merleau-Ponty's writings on 'precognitive familiarity' (Carman, 2008, p. 106) are perhaps most evident in Bourdieu's closely related concepts of 'practical sense' ('involvement in the world which presupposes no representation', see Bourdieu, 1990, p. 66) and 'habitus' (defined by Bourdieu, 1977, p. 72, as a set of 'durable, transposable dispositions' that are embodied). Indeed, in a discussion of 'bodily knowledge' ('knowledge that provides a practical comprehension of the world quite different from the ... decoding ... normally designated by the idea of comprehension', see Bourdieu, 2000, p. 135), he is quite explicit about the connections between his own work and that of Merleau-Ponty:

> The agent engaged in practice knows the world but ... as Merleau-Ponty showed ... knows it ... without objectifying distance, takes it for granted ... is caught up in it, bound up with it ... inhabits it like ... a familiar habitat ... feels at home.
>
> (ibid., pp. 142–3)

Elsewhere in the same discussion, Bourdieu (ibid., p. 152) proceeds to state that: 'The body is in the social world but the social world is in the body' (echoing Merleau-Ponty's assertions regarding the inseparability of inner subject and outer world).

So, given these direct parallels between Merleau-Ponty's philosophy and Bourdieu's social theory, what does Bourdieu see as the problem with phenomenological analysis that requires it to be sociologised? Furthermore, what might be involved in this sociologising of phenomenology?

Bourdieu's view is that it is necessary to sociologise phenomenological analysis because, while its account of a 'relationship of familiarity with the familiar environment' (Bourdieu, 1990, p. 25) is, as he puts it, 'indispensable' (Bourdieu, 2000, p. 146), phenomenology has tended not to deal with the historically and culturally specific conditions, including the social divisions, within which such relationships of 'familiarity' are formed. It has therefore come with a large measure of 'universalism'. This is the case not only in phenomenological philosophy but also in elements of phenomenological geography. For example, at one moment Seamon (1980, p. 148) defines the purpose of his geography as that of attending 'to the essential nature of ... dwelling on earth', and in the report of his empirical research on everyday environmental experience he claims that the descriptions provided by group members, who were of course living in historically and culturally specific conditions, 'reflect human experience in its typicality' (Seamon, 1979, p. 23). Still, it is by no means inevitable that phenomenological perspectives must operate at this universalistic level. On the contrary, there is no reason why phenomenology cannot pay greater attention to issues of social difference, so as to explore with greater specificity the diversity of human experiences. It is better, for instance, to speak of socially differentiated 'lifeworlds', in the plural, rather than to start out with the assumption that there can be any singular, universally shared realm of familiarity or sociability.

For Bourdieu, sociologising phenomenology involves identifying different types of habitus (different sets of embodied dispositions) that are related to different positions in society. From this starting point, then, 'implicit understanding' (Taylor, 2006, p. 212) and at-homeness (Seamon, 1979) are regarded as a particular 'coincidence between habitus and habitat' (Bourdieu, 2000, p. 147). For instance, Bourdieu (1977, pp. 81–2) is interested in forms of 'class habitus', referring to 'dispositions which are ... marks of social position', and which are also, of course, marks of social inequality (see especially Bourdieu, 1984, for his critical sociology of 'taste'). It is important to realise, though, that when he writes about embodied dispositions as 'marks of social position', this is not simply a theory of the determination of action by an external social structure. Bourdieu's focus on practices leads him to reject this sort of 'social physics', just as he wants to move beyond 'an unreconstructed phenomenology' (Bourdieu and Wacquant, 1992, pp. 7–9).

Simon Charlesworth's remarkable book, *A Phenomenology of Working Class Experience* (2000), which presents findings from his phenomenologically inspired fieldwork, carried out during the 1990s in a northern English town called Rotherham, serves to illustrate Bourdieu's point about a fit between 'habitus and habitat'. Charlesworth's study was very much informed by Bourdieu's social theory of practice, and it provides a helpful example of what it may mean to sociologise phenomenological analysis. Charlesworth (ibid., p. 23) insists 'that bodily experience cannot be studied apart from the cultures in which we become ... agents endowed with a form of corporeal generative knowing beyond the merely cognitive'. 'Understanding Rotherham', he argues, 'means understanding the habituated manner of comportment through which the place exists ... the sense that life has for Rotherham people ... their being-in-the-world' (ibid., pp. 92–3). His ethnography highlights the material conditions of 'economic necessity and dispossession' (ibid., p. 11) within which that being-in-the-world took shape, and, while such conditions of working-class living are obviously not confined solely to Rotherham in the 1990s, the account that he gives has a strong local-historical dimension. What I find useful about Charlesworth's book is that its concern is with those matters of dwelling or habitation (of sense of place) which have been central to this chapter, yet he approaches them in a way that is firmly committed to their historical and cultural grounding.

It is not just in sociology but also in philosophy that some of the limitations to Merleau-Ponty's work on embodiment have been acknowledged. In a recent commentary on Merleau-Ponty's writings that is generally supportive of his overall philosophical project, Lawrence Hass (2008, pp. 93–4) sees that:

> For Merleau-Ponty ... the body ... is our 'potentiality' ... in a field of possibilities. ... But ... there is another dimension which it would be folly to forget: the experiential field is also political. It is a site of force relations ... Merleau-Ponty ... is missing a 'body politics' – and this is a serious omission.

In making this criticism, Hass is drawing especially on feminist engagements with phenomenological philosophy, such as those found in the 'corporeal feminism' of Elizabeth Grosz (1994) and in Iris Young's classic essay on a phenomenology of 'feminine bodily existence' (Young, 2005 [1980], p. 30).

Grosz (1994, p. 19) contends that 'there is no body as such ... only bodies', preferring to speak in the plural rather than accepting the kind of universalistic references to 'the body' that are made by Merleau-Ponty. She points to 'his avoidance of the question of sexual difference and specificity' (ibid., p. 103), and goes so far as to suggest that 'his apparent generalizations regarding subjectivity ... in fact tend to take men's experiences for human ones'. Young's critique does concede that 'at the most basic descriptive level, Merleau-Ponty's account of the relation of the lived body to its world ... applies to any human existence in a general way' (Young, 2005 [1980], pp. 31–2), but, crucially, she continues: 'At a more specific level ... there is a particular style of ... feminine bodily comportment ... feminine being-in-the-world' (she is careful to qualify this reference to 'feminine being-in-the-world' with a reminder that her essay is restricted to a consideration of the experiences of many women in 'contemporary ... industrial, urban, and commercial society', and so it 'may not apply to the situation of women in other societies and other epochs', see ibid., p. 30). Her point of departure for discussing 'feminine bodily comportment' and bodily movement is an observation of the difference 'between the way boys and girls throw' (ibid., p. 32), and she proceeds to explore 'the most simple body orientations of men and women as they sit, stand, and walk'. Young (ibid., pp. 43–4) concludes that:

> The young girl acquires many subtle habits of ... comportment – walking like a girl ... standing and sitting like a girl, gesturing like a girl, and so on. ... The more a girl assumes her status as feminine ... the more she ... enacts her own body inhibition. ... While very young children show virtually no differences in motor skills, movement, spatial perception, etc., differences seem to appear ... in the process of growing up.

What this indicates is precisely the importance of a feminist 'body politics' (Hass, 2008, p. 94), despite what Meyrowitz (1985, p. 225) writes about electronic media and 'situational androgyny' (and see Bourdieu, 2000, p. 141, who also reflects on how 'the learning of masculinity and femininity tends to inscribe the difference ... in ... ways of walking, talking, standing, looking, sitting, etc.').

Finally here, in the light of these debates about gender and embodiment, it might be interesting to return to a topic discussed earlier, namely the uses (but also the non-uses) of media technologies in familiar material environments. In so doing, I want to recall some empirical research that was carried out back in the 1980s. Ann Gray's study of women's relationships to the video recorder (Gray, 1987, 1992) was concerned with the gendered meanings of what was then a new media technology in everyday living. Employing an inventive strategy in her interviews with thirty women (who happen to have lived in a part of the UK that is close to where Charlesworth's fieldwork was conducted), Gray (1987, p. 43) asked them 'to imagine pieces of equipment' in their households 'as coloured either pink or blue', with the aim of highlighting the 'gender specificity ... of domestic technology':

This produces almost uniformly pink irons and blue electric drills, with many interesting mixtures along the spectrum. ... VCRs and ... all home entertainment technology would seem to be a potentially lilac area, but my research has shown that we must break down the VCR into its different modes in our colour-coding. The 'record', 'rewind' and 'play' modes are usually lilac, but the timer switch is nearly always blue. ... The blueness of the timer is exceeded only by the deep indigo of the remote control ... which in all cases is held by the man.

That 'colour-coding' strategy can be seen to have illustrated the cultural significances of technologies-as-texts in household contexts (Silverstone, 1990, p. 189, refers to 'the texts of ... hardware'). However, I prefer to regard Gray's research as having been about, at least in part, the embodied practices and dispositions of media users, and about 'how meanings ... emerge from practices' (Anderson and Harrison, 2010b, p. 6). She paid careful attention, then, to the gendered practical competences, and also to a lack of technical know-how, involved in the uses or non-uses of 'technology in the domestic environment' (see especially Gray, 1992, pp. 164–90). For example, Gray (ibid., p. 179) notes 'that the video recorder timer switch seemed to present ... difficulties for the women', with male partners typically operating that device, yet 'many of their cookers ... had a time-setting function' that the women used 'without difficulty', and which 'very few of the men could operate'. This aspect of her work could clearly be linked to phenomenological analysis and the call to sociologise it (indeed, Gray does briefly consider Bourdieu's perspective on taste, see ibid., pp. 23–5).

Place and Placelessness

Alongside Tuan, Buttimer and Seamon, Relph (2008 [1976]) is another of those pioneers of phenomenological geography who developed a distinctive experiential perspective on formations of place in everyday living. One of his key contributions to the understanding of place as a practical and emotional accomplishment is the concept of 'existential insideness' (ibid., p. 55), which he defines as 'place ... experienced without deliberate and selfconscious reflection yet ... full with significances ... the insideness that most people experience when they are at home and in their own town or region'. Given his words 'when they are at home', it is worth noting that Seamon (1979, p. 90) makes the connection with his own notion of at-homeness, suggesting that existential insideness can be thought of as the 'most profound' form of at-homeness, where 'life holds continuity and regularity' and 'its mundane aspects ... are ... rarely reflected upon'. Interestingly, though, in detailing different modes of experiential involvement with environments, Relph (2008 [1976], p. 51) also proposed an opposing term, 'existential outsideness', arguing that this type of outsideness is marked by 'a sense of ... alienation ... of not belonging'. It may be felt, for example, 'by newcomers ... or by people who, having been away ... return to feel strangers' (Seamon and Sowers, 2008, pp. 45–6).

I find Relph's concept of existential outsideness to be a potentially fruitful one. Indeed, it will be used later in the book to help account for the initial experiences of some transnational migrants on arrival as 'newcomers' in a new country, interacting in and with a range of new settings (I am referring here to an empirical research project on the experiences of young people who moved from Eastern Europe to the UK in the mid-2000s, to be discussed at the close of the next chapter). However, I also find Relph's application of the concept to be partly problematic, because of the way in which he positions it within a much wider argument concerning the emergence of 'a placeless geography' (Relph, 2008 [1976], p. 117). It is to this wider argument that I turn now, and it means going back to the theme of placelessness which was introduced in the previous chapter via my critique of Meyrowitz's *No Sense of Place* (1985).

According to Relph (2008 [1976], p. 143), the growth of placelessness in contemporary living has involved a proliferation of 'anonymous spaces and exchangeable environments' that serve to undermine the constitution of 'significant places', and, more specifically, he believes that this 'undermining' is the result of particular developments in architecture, planning and technology. The main targets of his criticism of the built environment, then, are modernist 'International Style' urban structures made from concrete, steel and glass, along with locations that 'declare themselves unequivocally to be "Vacationland" or "Consumerland"' (ibid., pp. 92–3) and suburban residential estates with their seemingly 'endless subdivisions of identical houses' (ibid., p. 105). Above all, though, Relph (ibid., p. 90) sees the emergence of a placeless geography as the result of developments in 'mass communications'. His definition of mass communications includes, in addition to print media and broadcasting, a range of transportation sites and systems: 'Roads, railways, airports, cutting across or imposed on the landscape rather than developing with it, are not only features of placelessness in their own right, but ... have encouraged the spread of placelessness well beyond ... immediate impacts' (ibid.). Tellingly, in relation to physical transport, Relph (ibid., p. 83) sees technologically mediated mobility as the enemy of senses of place, contending that the 'meaning of "home" has been weakened ... through increased mobility'. Indeed, at one point Seamon (1979, p. 91) somewhat surprisingly adopts Relph's general line of argument on growing placelessness, declaring that: 'Today, in an era of mobility and mass communications ... technology and mass culture destroy the uniqueness of places and promote global homogenization.' Within this way of thinking, existential outsideness comes to be understood, at least in part, as the experience of 'not belonging' in 'anonymous spaces'.

The problem, from my perspective, is that the argument is flawed, and I believe it is possible to identify certain contradictions in the positions that are taken by Relph (2008 [1976]) and Seamon (1979). While the form and design of an environment do obviously have a bearing on its use, both Relph and Seamon, in their statements about placelessness, end up giving too much importance to architecture, planning and technology as determining forces (I would go so far as to suggest that they occasionally offer versions of environmental and technological determinism). The skyscraper, the holiday complex or shopping mall, the housing estate and the spaces of media or transportation are all regarded as somehow innately placeless and anonymous. Yet this goes against the grain of phenomenological geography's most significant insight, which is that the inhabitants of an environment can ultimately constitute it as a place by making themselves at home there through their repetitive, habitual practices. As Relph (2008 [1976], p. 123) himself puts it elsewhere in *Place and Placelessness*, it is 'the intentionality of experience' that gives environments a lived-in quality. In other words, to repeat a point made near the start of this chapter with reference to Tuan's work, places are locations made familiar, concrete and meaningful through practice. Furthermore, Seamon's own empirical research material, gathered in an American industrial city, includes a number of examples where media and transport technologies were being employed as resources in place-making activities. In those cases, technologically mediated mobility was not the enemy of senses of place. Rather, along with other habitual, everyday movements, it actually helped to facilitate at-homeness.

Non-places

Many of the same claims about increasing placelessness in contemporary society are repeated in the work of Augé (2009 [1995]). Indeed, much the same theoretical problem can be found there too (although, to be fair, he does make a helpful reference to de Certeau's pragmatics of everyday living, see ibid., p. 64). In general terms, Augé (ibid., p. 63) paints a bleak picture of 'a world ... surrendered to ... the fleeting ... the ephemeral ... where people are born in the clinic and die in hospital, where transit points and temporary abodes are proliferating'. As he indicates with the title of his book, his main concept is that of 'non-places':

> Non-places are the real measure of our time; one that could be quantified ... by totalling all the air, rail and motorway routes, the mobile cabins called 'means of transport' (aircraft, trains and road vehicles), the airports and railway stations, hotel chains, leisure parks, large retail outlets, and finally the complex skein of cable and wireless networks ... for the purposes of ... communication.
>
> (ibid.)

'The space of non-place', he summarises, is something that is only 'there to be passed through' (ibid., p. 83).

In addition, Augé (ibid., pp. xi–xii) echoes Seamon's sentiments regarding the destruction of 'the uniqueness of places' and the promotion of 'global homogenization':

> The spaces of circulation, consumption and communication are multiplying across the globe ... the same hotel chains, the same television networks are cinched tightly round the globe, so that we feel constrained by uniformity ... sameness ... and to cross international

borders brings no more profound variety than … walking between … rides at Disneyland.

Once again, I am proposing that the argument is flawed. There are strong hints here of the environmental and technological determinism found in parts of Relph (2008 [1976]) and Seamon (1979). Augé has a tendency to make assumptions about how 'we feel' in these so-called non-places, without having investigated people's (socially differentiated) environmental experiences of, say, 'hotel chains', 'television networks' or 'airports'. Since the airport might justifiably be seen as Augé's main example of a non-place (the story of a trip to an airport to catch an international flight features in his prologue to *Non-places*, see Augé, 2009 [1995], pp. 1–5), I want to look more closely at this example with the help of Tomlinson (1999) and Cresswell (2006).

While Tomlinson (1999, p. 111) acknowledges that Augé has identified 'genuinely new … cultural-spatial phenomena' with reference to international air terminals and other contemporary sites of 'transit', he also emphasises the point that 'the sort of locales Augé describes do not … map the totality of modern … experience'. So, for instance, Tomlinson (ibid., p. 6) insists that: 'To decide whether the homogenization thesis really obtains you have to venture outside … the terminal.' Later in my book, when I discuss empirical research findings on the environmental experiences of trans-European migrants, it will be evident that crossing international borders can bring considerably 'more profound variety than … walking between … rides at Disneyland' (Augé, 2009 [1995], p. xii). Moreover, Tomlinson (1999, pp. 111–12) argues convincingly that experiences of airports are likely to be highly varied, and that Augé 'does not account for … the … experience of … the check-in clerks, baggage handlers, cleaners, caterers, security staff and so forth', for whom 'the terminal is clearly a … place – their workplace'.

Cresswell (2006, pp. 219–58) goes further still in developing a critique of Augé's book, and his critical engagement with the concept of non-places is based on a case study of Schiphol Airport in Amsterdam. Whereas Augé's account of air travel presents a singular image of the passenger, Cresswell (ibid., p. 223) writes of the 'differentiated traveler' (of distinctions between groups of passengers, from the 'global kinetic elite' to 'budget airline flyers … refugees, and asylum seekers'). Like Tomlinson, he also realises that an airport is a 'workplace' for some, listing 'flight attendants' and 'mechanics' as well as 'check-in workers, janitors' (ibid.) and 'taxi drivers' (ibid., pp. 252–4). Concluding his case study, Cresswell (ibid., p. 257) observes that:

It does not do justice to the many-layered complexity of ... Schiphol ... to call it a non-place. ... Schiphol is a ... space on which an intricate 'place-ballet' of multiple movements takes place on a daily basis. ... Schiphol may be a node in a global space of flows, but it is still uniquely Schiphol.

The brief mention in this quote of a 'space of flows' serves to signal the way forward to my next chapter, where that concept resurfaces in a discussion of Manuel Castells's theory of 'the network society' (Castells, 1996). However, for the purposes of the present chapter, Cresswell's key reference is to Seamon's notion of place choreographies, and his view is that even at a transit point like Schiphol Airport there remains the potential for a certain uniqueness of place to be formed.

3 Forms of Dwelling in a World of Flux

My principal aim in the previous chapter was to establish an understanding of place that addresses issues of habit, affect and attachment to environment in everyday living. In attempting to establish such an understanding, which I take to be crucial, I made reference to important work across a range of academic disciplines in the social sciences and humanities, and I devoted a considerable number of words to this since few students in the field of media studies are likely to be familiar with the phenomenology of familiarity. Reviewing selected phenomenological perspectives enabled me to link formations of place with several different sorts of mobility (walking, driving, typing, keypad pressing, mouse manoeuvring and double-clicking, moving around in media settings and so on). Towards the end of that second chapter, I discussed the view of certain theorists (notably Relph, 2008 [1976]; Augé, 2009 [1995]) that developments in media and transportation have weakened senses of place and experiences of at-homeness. They argue that these technological developments contribute to an increasingly placeless existence, and there are therefore some parallels with Joshua Meyrowitz's account of social change (Meyrowitz, 1985), which was dealt with in detail back in the first chapter. Contesting their claims, I preferred to see technologically mediated mobility, alongside other types of everyday movement, as significant for the constitution of places. For example, I much preferred David Seamon's empirical data, which include fragments of material on everyday media uses, to the argument he borrows from Edward Relph, that place-making is threatened with destruction today 'in an era of mobility and mass communications' (Seamon, 1979, p. 91). In this third chapter, which is a little shorter than the one preceding it, I continue to explore the relations between place and mobility (and to venture beyond the usual boundaries of media studies). My main focus here, though, will be on approaches that are concerned with transnational mobilities and local–global intersections. I will be asking, in David Morley's words, 'how, in a world of flux, forms of ... dwelling are sustained and reinvented' (Morley, 2000, p. 13), hence the phrase in the chapter's title. Questions about the transnational were raised in my critical discussion of notions of placelessness, where the problematic idea of global homogenisation was mentioned. However, the answers that are provided over the coming pages offer a more nuanced account of contemporary globalising processes than that which is found either in *Place and Placelessness* (Relph, 2008 [1976]) or in *Non-places* (Augé, 2009 [1995]).

Dwelling and Travelling

I want to begin my review of work in this chapter by looking at James Clifford's seminal essay on 'traveling cultures' (see Clifford, 1997, pp. 17–46, for material that initially appeared as Clifford, 1992). My reasons for beginning with his essay are, first, because it helped to put the matter of mobilities, including what John Urry (2000, p. 66; see also Urry, 2007, p. 169) names the 'imaginative travel' of television viewing, on the theoretical agenda (on the methodological agenda too), and, second, because of the way in which he insists there on a combined cultural analysis of 'practices of dwelling and traveling' (Clifford, 1997, p. 36). Indeed, Clifford's insistence on the need for a joint consideration of 'dwelling and traveling' has influenced, at least in part, my own decision to bring themes of place and mobility together in the same book.

The point of departure for Clifford's essay is a critical reflection on certain traditional ethnographic research strategies that have been employed in the discipline of anthropology. More specifically, his interest is in how anthropologists have traditionally seen their objects of study in particular 'spatial terms': 'Villages, inhabited by natives ... bounded sites ... for intensive visiting by anthropologists ... have long served as ... mappable centers for the community, and by extension, the culture' (ibid., pp. 19–21). Construing anthropological 'fieldwork' in this way, primarily 'as a practice of co-residence' (ibid., p. 21) in 'bounded sites', 'rather than of travel' by researchers who are moving across the globe, involves leaving other significant things 'out of the ethnographic frame':

> The means of transport is largely erased – the boat, the land rover, the mission airplane. These technologies suggest systematic prior and ongoing contacts and commerce with exterior places and forces which are not part of the field/object ... 'being there' ... is separated from ... travel ('getting there') ... movement in and out of the field

by ... anthropologists ... and ... natives. Generally speaking, what's hidden is the wider global world of intercultural import–export in which the ethnographic encounter is always already enmeshed.

(ibid., p. 23)

As becomes clear in this passage, Clifford is not only concerned with the travelling that is done by researchers. Anthropologists and 'natives' are positioned differently in relation to movement, as well as in relation to residence, but some of the latter may increasingly be travelling long distances, and so he proceeds to ask why it is that anthropologists do not 'focus on any culture's farthest range of travel while also looking at its centers, its villages, its intensive fieldsites' (ibid., p. 25). The key terms here, though, are 'while also', since his goal is 'not to replace the cultural figure "native" with the intercultural figure "traveler"' (ibid., p. 24), but rather to recommend 'that the specific dynamics of dwelling/traveling be understood'. 'This is not nomadology', he confirms (ibid., p. 42). Nevertheless, precisely as a consequence of increased transnational mobilities, or of what he calls 'the wider global world of intercultural import–export', ideas about dwelling and boundary do now have 'to be reconceived' (ibid., p. 44). In other words, it is necessary to consider the changing forms of dwelling in a world of flux. I should stress that this must not mean leaving behind crucial issues of habit, affect and attachment to environment in everyday living. Nor, for that matter, does it mean forgetting about important issues to do with situational geography and electronically mediated communication. It does require, however, that far greater attention is paid to 'movement in and out' of environments (that is, to the comings and goings that Ingold, 2007, p. 2, identifies as significant elements of place-making in social life).

While I have described Clifford's essay as seminal work (and I stand by this), there were other academics in the 1990s who made similar points about the way in which anthropologists had traditionally seen their objects of study as cultures in bounded sites. For instance, social anthropologist Ulf Hannerz (1996, p. 4), in his book *Transnational Connections: Culture, People, Places*, reflects on the character of the discipline that he 'turned to' as a university student back in the 1960s: 'this was the subject ... where the assumption ... was that ... you would end up in a distant village in another continent, trying to make sense of ... local life'. 'The world ... to anthropologists', he explains, 'seemed to be made up of a myriad of such ... local, bounded entities; a sort of global mosaic' (ibid.). As Hannerz (ibid., p. 3) neatly expresses it, though, 'boundaries ... are not what they used to be'. There is consequently a need, in his view, 'to cultivate new understandings of ... transnational connections' (ibid., p. 4). Suspicious of the notion of a 'global mosaic', he proposes the concept of a 'global ecumene' (see ibid., pp. 6–7; also Hannerz, 2001), which better conveys, for him, the complex 'interconnectedness of the world' (and see the case made by fellow Scandinavian anthropologists, Olwig and Hastrup, 1997, who refer to Hannerz's concept of a global ecumene in their related discussion of 'the shifting anthropological object').

Similarly, Arjun Appadurai (1996, pp. 48–9) calls for a 'transnational anthropology', arguing that there are social changes on a global scale which 'ethnography must confront':

> As groups migrate, regroup in new locations ... and reconfigure their ethnic projects, the 'ethno' in ethnography takes on a slippery ... quality, to which the descriptive practices of ethnography will have to respond. The landscapes of group identity – the ethnoscapes – around the world are no longer familiar anthropological objects ... tightly territorialized, spatially bounded. ... There is an urgent need to focus on the cultural dynamics of ... deterritorialization.

Before long, I will be returning to Appadurai's last word there, 'deterritorialization', but for now I want to consider more broadly what he has to say about physical migration and the shifting 'landscapes of group identity'. Like Clifford (see especially Clifford, 1997, pp. 244–77), Appadurai has a strong interest in the formation of contemporary 'diaspora cultures' (ibid., p. 36).

Two features of Appadurai's argument are particularly relevant to the unfolding concerns of my book. The first of these has to do with the connection he makes between migration and media, or between what he terms 'ethnoscapes' and 'mediascapes' (see Appadurai, 1996, pp. 33–6). He defines ethnoscapes as 'the landscape of persons who constitute the shifting world in which we live ... immigrants, refugees, exiles, guest workers, and other moving groups and individuals' (ibid., p. 33; and note that such 'other moving groups and individuals' can still be seen to include anthropologists). Meanwhile, the concept of mediascapes is employed to refer to the circulation of electronically mediated sounds and images (part of what Clifford, 1997, p. 28, calls the 'forces that pass ... through'), not just at the local and national levels but increasingly on a global scale. Appadurai's interest is precisely in how 'moving' people, who have regrouped 'in new locations', encounter these circulating sounds and images:

Turkish guest workers in Germany watch Turkish films in their German flats ... Koreans in Philadelphia watch the ... Olympics in Seoul through satellite feeds ... and Pakistani cabdrivers in Chicago listen to cassettes of sermons recorded in mosques in Pakistan or Iran. ... The story of mass migrations (voluntary and forced) is hardly a new feature of human history. But when it is juxtaposed with the rapid flow of mass-mediated images ... we have a new order ... of modern subjectivities.

(Appadurai, 1996, p. 4)

Appadurai (ibid.) regards this historically distinctive encounter or juxta-position as contributing not only to the constitution of 'a new order ... of modern subjectivities' but also to the creation of 'diasporic public spheres', which are geographically dispersed beyond national frontiers. The specific examples of listening and viewing that he gives here are good ones, particularly as an illustration of transnational and diasporic communications, and yet the social circumstances in which 'ethnic projects' get reconfigured are more complex still. For instance, it might be helpful to think, in addition, about the implications for 'group iden-tity' when young 'Punjabi Londoners' avidly follow an Australian soap opera broadcast on British terrestrial television, or else when Punjabi households in the UK view 'video letters' recorded and sent by extended family members from South Asia and North America (both of these examples are drawn from Gillespie, 1995). Indeed, the last of these examples, like the last of Appadurai's, which was that of 'Pakistani cabdrivers' in the US listening to 'cassettes of sermons recorded ... in Pakistan or Iran', serves to demonstrate that 'small media' (Dayan, 1999, pp. 22–3) have played an important part in diasporic communi-cations alongside 'conventional' or 'mass' media. Of course, it is more likely nowadays, depending on access to the necessary technology, that interpersonal audiovisual communication between family members on different continents will be conducted via the internet.

A second, closely related feature of Appadurai's argument that I want to highlight is his assertion that: 'The globalization of culture is not the same as its homogenization' (Appadurai, 1996, p. 42). Clearly, this asser-tion contradicts the claims of Relph and Augé concerning the global spread of 'uniformity', and therefore of placelessness or non-places. Writers like Hannerz (1996, 2001) and Appadurai (1996) choose instead to emphasise heterogeneity, although it is vital to see that this hetero-geneity involves more than simply the old differences of a global mosaic. In a global ecumene, then, transnational connections help give rise to new and distinctive cultural mixes or 'confluences' in a myriad of local (but far from bounded) social settings, and so 'there is still ample room for the deep study of specific geographies … and … histories' (ibid., p. 17; see also Hall, 1992, p. 310, on contemporary 'cultures of hybridity'; Gillespie, 2002, p. 188, on 'cross-cultural navigations'). However, an important qualification to add here is that the 'deep study' of which Appadurai writes may increasingly demand 'multi-sited ethnographies' (Gillespie, 2000, p. 170) and 'mobile methods' (Urry, 2007, pp. 29–30; see also Büscher *et al.*, 2011; Fincham *et al.*, 2010) of research.

Let me come back now to Clifford's essay on travelling cultures, because, in continuing to explore the question of how forms of dwelling 'are sustained and reinvented' (Morley, 2000, p. 13) in a world of flux, I would like to pick up on some of the things that he has to say there about 'dwelling-in-travel' (Clifford, 1997, p. 26). He presents what he describes as 'an extreme case' of such dwelling-in-travel, which is that of 'a group of veteran performers who play Hawaiian guitar, sing, and dance', and whose 'experience has been one of almost uninterrupted travel', since they have spent 'fifty-six years on the road, almost never going back to Hawaii' (ibid., pp. 25–6). 'How', asks Clifford (ibid., p. 26), 'did they preserve and invent a sense of Hawaiian "home"?' This is evidently an uncommon case of constant physical travelling, a story of lives being lived 'on the road'. Yet although these 'veteran performers' must surely have been touched in numerous ways by their physical movements through 'the Far East, South Asia, the Middle East, North Africa … Europe, and the United States' (ibid., p. 25), the focus of their own particular ethnic 'project', which is bound up with their style of musical performance, seems to have been on the doing of 'Hawaiianness' (ibid., p. 44). Drawing on Pierre Bourdieu's terms, which I discussed in the previous chapter, Clifford (ibid.) conceptualises this long-term maintenance and reproduction of 'a sense of Hawaiian "home"' (while living 'away') as 'something … like a habitus, a set of practices and dispositions … which could be remembered, articulated in specific contexts'.

By briefly considering a very different example, which typically involves physical movement on a far smaller scale, I hope to show that it is possible to extend Clifford's notion of dwelling-in-travel, in order to allow for a fuller understanding of the common uses of mobile media technologies. I am thinking, in particular, about everyday practices of mobile-phone communication, and about a social phenomenon that Morley (2003) names 'the dislocation of domesticity'. This 'dislocation', which also implies a degree of relocation and an activity of place-making in media spaces, entails a technological mobilisation of at-homeness:

'one of the things that the mobile phone does is to dislocate the idea of home ... the mobile phone ... is ... allowing us to take our homes ... the chatter of the hearth ... with us' (ibid., pp. 451–3). A related example of this sort of dwelling-in-travel would be the experience reported by one of Michael Bull's research participants, who was quoted earlier in the book: 'When I get in my car and I turn on my radio ... I'm already home' (Bull, 2001, p. 185).

Finally here, as promised, I return to the concept of deterritorialisation employed by Appadurai (1996). When he points to the 'urgent need to focus on the cultural dynamics of ... deterritorialization' (ibid., p. 49), he tends to link this term with his discussion of physical migration and diaspora cultures. However, for a broader application of the concept, I want to refer to John Tomlinson's book, *Globalization and Culture* (1999). Tomlinson (ibid., p. 9) certainly accepts that transnational physical travel, including migration, has been significant for globalising processes, but he also stresses that it is necessary 'not to exaggerate the way long-distance travel figures ... in the lives of the majority of people in the world'. For him, as for Morley (2000, p. 14), it is 'in the transformation of localities ... that ... globalisation ... has its most important expression'. As Tomlinson (1999, p. 9) observes, 'the paradigmatic experience of global modernity for most people' (and that would include most migrants, following their physical relocation) is still one of 'local life', but it is a form of local living in which 'global modernity' brings a range of things 'to them'. This is what he chooses to call 'the mundane experience of deterritorialization' (ibid., p. 113), in which 'our daily lives become more and more interwoven with, and penetrated by, influences ... that have their origins far away' (see also Giddens, 1990, p. 19, on the 'phantasmagoric' character of 'locales' in contemporary society). Media and communication technologies clearly play a part in that interweaving or intersection of the local and the global, and, according to Tomlinson (1999, p. 116), such technologies provide both '"entrances into" ... and ... "exits from" ... our intimate living spaces'. On the one hand, they bring an 'intrusion of distant events' (Giddens, 1991, p. 27) into the everyday, while, on the other hand, they are simultaneously affording their users the feeling of being 'transported' elsewhere.

A Global Sense of Place

Following on directly from my closing remarks in the previous section, let me pursue that point about globalisation and 'the transformation of localities' (Morley, 2000, p. 14). I want to do so by considering some important arguments made by human geographer Doreen Massey (see especially Massey, 1994, 1995, 2005), who calls for 'a rethinking of the concept of place' (Massey, 1994, p. 120) to fit contemporary social circumstances. In particular, I will be reflecting on her ideas about a 'global' sense of place (about 'what happens to the notion of place now, in this age of globalization', see Massey, 1995, p. 46).

Broadly in line with the critiques of traditional anthropological field-work offered by Clifford (1992, 1997), Hannerz (1996) and Appadurai (1996), Massey is suspicious of attempts to conceptualise places as 'bounded entities'. She writes of 'the openness of places' (Massey, 1995, pp. 59–61), having rejected 'assumptions ... of place as closed' (Massey, 2005, p. 6) at an early stage in her thinking about the concept:

> And so the question became how to abandon this understanding of 'place' and yet retain an appreciation of specificity, of uniqueness ... how ... we might engage the 'local', the 'regional', while at the same time insisting on internationalism. It was in this context that I worked towards what I would come to call 'a global sense of place'.
>
> (ibid., p. 196)

For Massey, then, globalising processes are not eliminating local 'uniqueness'. She sees that, as Appadurai (1996, p. 42) puts it, 'global-ization ... is not the same as ... homogenization' (for a very similar statement, see Massey, 1994, p. 156). Indeed, she realises, in a way which closely parallels Hannerz's ideas about a global ecumene (Hannerz, 1996, 2001), that this specificity or uniqueness is partly a consequence of transnational connections: 'The ... particularity of any place is ... constructed ... precisely (in part) through the specificity of links and interconnections to ... "beyond" ... the global as part of what constitutes the local ... place is ... open and porous' (Massey, 1994, p. 5; and see Cresswell, 2002, pp. 25–6, on Massey as a theorist who has been able 'to think through the place/mobility dualism in ... sophisticated ... ways' by approaching places 'as open and permeable').

As I have presented them so far, Massey's ideas about a global sense of place (and about the openness of places) may seem rather abstract. One of the great strengths of her work, though, is the range of examples that she employs to illustrate her theoretical arguments. For instance, in a recent book (Massey, 2007) she discusses the case of London, the 'world city' that she has lived in for many years. In her introduction to this book, Massey (ibid., p. 13) poses what she regards as a standard geographical question about how the city's boundaries might best be 'drawn', asking 'where does London end?' However, her answer (or, to be precise, her doubt about the validity of the question) is far from standard:

> But maybe space ... does not work like that anymore (if it ever did). Maybe places do not lend themselves to having lines drawn around them. (London is an extreme example – a good laboratory for the argument – but this is a general point.) ... There is a vast geography of dependencies, relations ... that spreads out from here around the globe. This is ... to argue that, in considering ... the practices, and the very character, of this place, it is necessary to follow also the lines of its engagement with elsewhere. Such lines of engagement are ... part of what makes it what it is.
>
> (ibid.)

More specifically, Massey (1994, pp. 152–4) has given an account of a walk through her own district of London, focusing on its 'local shopping centre ... Kilburn High Road', as a way of starting to show the distinctive mix of its 'links and interconnections to ... "beyond"'. Kilburn is, she states, a location 'for which I have a great affection', and, she insists, it 'certainly has "a character of its own"', yet it is 'impossible even to begin thinking about Kilburn High Road without bringing into play half the world and a considerable amount of British imperialist history' (ibid., pp. 153–4). For example, there is 'the newspaper stand' that displays 'papers from every county of what my neighbours ... still often call the Irish Free State', while 'across the road ... there's a shop which as long as I can remember has displayed saris in the window ... life-sized models of Indian women ... and reams of cloth' (ibid., pp. 152–3). 'On the door', Massey (ibid., p. 153) continues, 'a notice announces a forthcoming concert ... Rekha, live, with Aamir Khan, Salman Khan, Jahi Chawla and Raveena Tandon.'

Evidently, the main point being made in that description of Kilburn High Road, as in the wider case of London as a world city, has to do with 'the lines of its engagement with elsewhere' (Massey, 2007, p. 13), such as the imported newspapers and visiting performers, which are 'part of what makes it what it is'. There is a further point, though, and it concerns what Massey (1994, p. 153) is calling Kilburn's unique 'character': 'while Kilburn may have a character of its own, it is absolutely not a seamless, coherent identity, a single sense of place which everyone shares'. Rather, she contends that it might be helpful to conceptualise her local area as having 'multiple identities' (ibid.), which are related to people's very different 'favourite haunts within it' and to 'the connections they make (physically, or by phone or post, or in memory and imagination) between here and the rest of the world'. This argument of Massey's, which is basically about accounting for differences, takes me back to one of the concerns of my previous chapter, where I considered Bourdieu's proposal for phenomenological analysis to be sociologised (Bourdieu and Wacquant, 1992).

Unlike Bourdieu, and also unlike the phenomenological geographers in her own discipline, Massey is not particularly influenced by phenomenological philosophy. Instead, her main theoretical and political points of departure for the study of practices are those of Marxism and feminism (it is worth noting that her ideas about a global sense of place had originally been aired in *Marxism Today*, see Massey, 1991; and the book in which that initial essay was later reprinted is entitled *Space, Place and Gender*, see Massey, 1994). Nevertheless, the interest that she has in analysing the multiple identities of places ('senses of place' in the plural) does broadly align her approach with Bourdieu's social theory, since both Massey and Bourdieu are keen to emphasise issues of social difference and power. I will be returning, at the end of the current section, to the relationship between Massey's work on place and that done by the phenomenological geographers.

Another example, this time of rural settings rather than an urban environment, can be found in Massey's account of the different social groups living in 'small villages set in the countryside around the city of Cambridge' (Massey, 1995, pp. 59–61; see also Massey, 2005, pp. 177–9). Drawing on the findings of an empirical research project, she identifies four such groups in these country villages, exploring what she refers to as their varied 'activity spaces':

> There are high-tech scientists, mainly men, whose work is based in Cambridge, though they often have computers with modem links at home as well. The companies they work for operate in a highly internationalized part of the economy, and these employees spend their time in constant contact with, and physically travelling between, colleagues and customers all around the world. ... At the other extreme are people who have never been to London and only rarely ... made it as far as Cambridge ... usually in order to go to the shops or ... to the hospital. These are the people who ... work locally – some on the farms, some in the village shops and services. ... There are other groups, too, in a sense in-between these two in terms of ... spatiality. There are people who work more or less locally ... nearby

or in Cambridge – maybe as cleaners or caterers ... for firms which are multinational. ... There are women who are the partners of the high-tech men, some of them presently at home with small children ... often being the heart and soul of local meetings and charities. For shopping, they are more likely to drive into Cambridge ... for holidays they may fly off to somewhere exotic; and they may have family in other parts of the country, whom they visit regularly and who visit them.

(Massey, 1995, pp. 59–60)

What this lengthy passage illustrates very well are the dynamics of class and gender that can emerge when investigating issues of 'spatiality', and especially when investigating the spatial reach (Buttimer, 1980) of people's activities. Although the members of the four groups identified by Massey all had a physical base in the same rural area, the 'stretching out' of their physical movements, and of their electronically mediated interpersonal communications, was highly varied and uneven.

Still, it is crucial to remember that, even for those village 'locals' (Massey, 1995, p. 59) who are more rooted than 'routed' (see Clifford, 1997), there remains the question of what transnational connections were bringing to them. As Massey (1995, p. 60) expresses it: 'Even the most "local" ... people ... have their lives touched by wider events ... farms ... may be affected by European legislation passed in Brussels ... nobody in the first world these days lives ... completely locally.' In addition to the farmworkers who may have been 'touched' by 'European legislation', it is not difficult to see how the jobs of 'cleaners or caterers' might have been affected by 'a geography of power' (ibid., p. 55), in which decisions taken thousands of miles away in the 'head office' of a multinational firm can touch the lives of people in Cambridgeshire villages (and, of course, there is the more general 'intrusion' of distant events via radio, television, newspapers and other media, see Giddens, 1991, p. 27).

Massey's commitment to addressing issues of social difference and power is perhaps at its strongest when she writes about 'the power geometry of time-space compression' (1994, p. 149). The concept of 'time-space compression' is associated with the work of a fellow (critical) human geographer, David Harvey (1989), who was interested in understanding, among other things, contemporary globalising processes. As Harvey (ibid., p. 240) explains, 'I use the word "compression" because ... capitalism has been characterized by speed-up in the pace of life, while so overcoming spatial barriers that the world some-times seems to collapse inwards upon us', and he goes on to propose that 'we have been experiencing ... an intense phase of time-space compression' (ibid., p. 284). While Massey (1995, p. 57) accepts that there is much evidence which 'would seem to support the thesis of increasing time-space compression', including clear evidence of a 'speed-up' in the sphere of media and communications, her difficulty is with the collective 'we have been experiencing' in Harvey's formula-tion, because: 'Different social groups ... are located in many different ways in the new organization of ... time-space' (Massey, 1994, p. 164; for precisely the same reason, it would be preferable to speak about 'mundane experiences' of deterritorialisation in the plural). Indeed, this is only one of several difficulties that Massey has with Harvey's perspec-tive on global social change (see also their contributions to Bird *et al.*, 1993; and for a helpful discussion of their theoretical and political disagreements, see Cresswell, 2004, pp. 53–75).

In Massey's reflections on the power geometry of time-space compression, she employs, once again, a number of examples to illus-trate her position, and she also identifies, once again, particular social groups whose members have very different experiences of spatiality and mobility:

> In a sense at the end of all the spectra are those who are ... doing the moving and the communicating and who are in some way in a posi-tion of control in relation to it – the jet-setters, the ones ... holding the international conference calls, the ones distributing the films, controlling the news, organizing the investments and the interna-tional currency transactions. ... But there are also groups ... doing a lot of physical moving ... who are not 'in charge' of the process in the same way at all ... the ... migrant workers ... crowding into Tijuana to make a perhaps fatal dash for it across the border into the US. ... And there are those ... who come half way round the world only to get held up in an interrogation room at Heathrow. Or – a different case again ... the ... pensioner in a bed-sit ... eating British working-class-style fish and chips from a Chinese take-away, watch-ing a US film on a Japanese television, and not daring to go out after dark.
>
> (Massey, 1994, pp. 149–50)

Note here that the 'power geometry' does not just involve a division between those who are physically on the move and those who are staying put (for instance, 'in a bed-sit ... not daring to go out after dark'), important though this division is. There is also the matter of 'differentiated mobility' (ibid., p. 149). In other words, there is a contrast between, for example, 'the jet-setters' and those who are, in Massey's account, 'held up in an interrogation room at Heathrow' (and see Cresswell, 2006, p. 223, for a similar point about the differentiated traveller in airport settings). Both groups are engaged in physical travelling, then, but there are clear 'differences in the ... degree of control' (Massey, 1994, p. 150) that they exercise over their movements (on differentiated mobility, see also Bauman, 1998, pp. 92–3, for his interesting distinction between 'tourists' and 'vagabonds').

Massey's mentioning of national borders and immigration policing leads me now to a brief but significant qualification that she makes with regard to her ideas about the 'openness' or permeability of places. Having argued that 'places do not lend themselves to having lines drawn around them', she nevertheless acknowledges the fact that 'boundaries matter' as 'one means of organizing social space' (Massey, 1995, p. 68): 'Where you live in relation to them determines the level of your local taxes ... where you were born in relation to them determines ... your nationality, determines which boundaries you may cross and those ... you may not.' As I indicated in the previous chapter with reference to the work of David Sibley (1995) and Lori Kendall (2002), theories of the permeability of the local, or of the regional and the national, must not rule out the possibility that place-making (at various geographical scales) might involve exclusionary practices.

To conclude this section of the chapter, I want to say something about the relationship between Massey's approach and that of the phenomenological geographers (especially Tuan, 1977; Seamon, 1979), whose writings were reviewed earlier in my book. I have already indicated that her main theoretical points of departure were not the same as theirs, but there is more to say by way of a comparison between the perspectives on offer. My own view is that Massey's global-sense-of-place thesis represents a valuable addition to previous work on place in human geography. In particular, her argument that the conceptualisation of place must take account of an 'intersection' (Massey, 1994, p. 154) of local and global social relations is a crucial one (as is her related moral argument about the importance of '"outwardlooking-ness" ... a positivity and aliveness to the world beyond one's own turf', see Massey, 2005, p. 15; although it ought to be remembered that Tuan, 1996, has advanced a related case for cosmopolitanism). However, despite Massey's many references to practice (and her citing of Thrift's non-representational theory, see Massey, 2005, p. 75; also Anderson, 2008, for a non-representational theorist's assessment of her work), I believe that what is missing from her approach to place is precisely a detailed attention to environmental experience, and to matters of dwelling or habitation. This can be found, of course, in the writings of Tuan and Seamon (as well as in phenomenological philosophy, see especially Heidegger, 1962, 1993 [1971]; Merleau-Ponty, 2002 [1962]), to which I will return in the final section of the chapter. Implicitly, Massey (2005, p. 6) is associating phenomenological geography with those notions of 'place as closed' that she has long sought to counter, and yet I can see no reason, in principle, why a concern with habitation and embodied practices should be at odds with an interest in the openness of places or in contemporary transnational connections. Both of these are necessary for coming to terms with forms of dwelling in a world of flux.

Space of Flows/Places

At the end of the previous chapter, reference was made to Schiphol Airport in Amsterdam as 'a node in a global space of flows' (Cresswell, 2006, p. 257), and I turn now to the distinction made by a well-known sociologist and communications researcher, Manuel Castells (1996, p. 423), between what he calls the space of flows and the 'space of places'. Over recent years, Castells's book, *The Rise of the Network Society*, which is the first book in his trilogy on 'the information age', has been widely cited across the social sciences and humanities, and, partly because his account of the network society closely associates global social change with developments in media and communications technology, it has been of considerable interest to many theorists in media (and cultural) studies (for example, see McGuigan, 1999, pp. 104–21; Webster, 2002, pp. 97–123; Hassan, 2004; van Dijk, 2006; Bell, 2007). Since Castells (1996), in the context of his rise-of-the-network-society thesis, deals with issues that are central to my current chapter (globalisation, transnational mobilities and their consequences for the constitution of places), his arguments there are also of interest to me (as are his subsequent reflections on 'the transformation of sociability' in contemporary society, Castells, 2001, pp. 125–33; and see Wittel, 2008, on the idea of 'a network sociality'). However, in focusing attention on his 'social theory of space' (Castells, 1996, p. 410) in this section, I will be concentrating on what I regard as significant problems with the way in which he deals with place and mobility, or with the relations between places and flows.

Space is defined by Castells (ibid., p. 411), in broad terms, as 'the material support of time-sharing social practices', although he stresses the point that 'simultaneous practices' today do not necessarily rely on the physical 'contiguity' of participants in social interaction. Indeed, for him, 'it is fundamental that we separate the basic concept of material support of simultaneous practices from the notion of contiguity' (ibid.; see also Thompson, 1995, p. 32, for a related discussion of the 'altered experience of simultaneity' or 'sense of now' in conditions of global modernity). This is because there is, in Castells's view, a new spatial form that he names the space of flows, which he believes is characteristic of the network society (for his general definition of 'the concept of network' as 'a set of interconnected nodes', and for the specific example of 'the global network of the new media', see Castells, 1996, pp. 470–1). He contends, then, that 'our society is constructed around flows: flows of capital, flows of information ... flows of organizational interaction, flows of images ... sounds' (ibid., pp. 411–12), and he sees these various flows as having been facilitated by the social development of technologies such as 'microelectronics, telecommunications, computer processing, broadcasting systems, and high-speed transportation' (ibid., p. 412; see also Castells *et al.*, 2007, p. 171, on how 'mobile communication technology greatly contributes to the spread of the space of flows').

It is at the stage where Castells (1996, pp. 412–13) is introducing his concept of the space of flows that he first reflects on the consequences of flows (or what Urry, 2000, 2007, also calls mobilities) for some places in the network society:

> The space of flows is not placeless ... places do not disappear, but their logic and meaning become absorbed in the network ... no place exists by itself ... places are the nodes of the network ... the location of strategically important functions.

The particular example with which he goes on to illustrate this argument is that of 'the global ... financial system' (Castells, 1996, p. 413). So in what he terms 'the network of global financial flows' (ibid., p. 470), the 'nodes of the network' are locations such as 'stock exchange markets, and their ancillary advanced services centers' around the world. Similarly, going back to an example of Tim Cresswell's with which I opened this section of my chapter, it is possible to think of Schiphol Airport as one of the major nodes in the network of international air travel (although, unlike Cresswell, 2006, p. 257, Castells has nothing to say about the intricate place choreographies that may be performed in social settings such as airports).

On the face of it, the case that Castells is advancing here would seem to have much in common with Massey's ideas about a global sense of place (Massey, 1994). Like her, he makes it clear that 'places do not disappear' in circumstances of globalisation, and, again like her, he looks to understand place relationally (that is, in terms of 'lines of ... engagement with elsewhere', Massey, 2007, p. 13). In the context of his remarks about the international financial system, he even discusses the example of 'global cities' (Castells, 1996, p. 413), prefiguring certain aspects of her analysis of London in *World City* (Massey, 2007). Still, having noted those similarities between the theoretical perspectives of Castells and Massey (and there are further points of overlap to which I will come shortly), I want to suggest that Massey's account of the openness of places in 'this age of globalization' (Massey, 1995, p. 46) is the more coherent and convincing. My reasons for suggesting this can be explained by examining what Castells (1996, pp. 423–8) writes about his concept of the space of places.

When Castells (ibid., pp. 412–13) states that places are 'nodes', with 'their logic and meaning' becoming 'absorbed in the network', it is crucial to understand that he is referring only to particular types of location, which, as he puts it, have 'strategically important functions' in relation to the space of flows. Indeed, he does not count these node-locations as being part of what he calls the space of places. Given the likelihood of confusion over this point, let me try to show the distinction that Castells is making, between the space of flows and the space of places, but also between places as nodes in a network and other kinds of location that he thinks of as being outside the 'global space of flows'. Of course, it is worth noting that, on either side of the distinction, he is still operating with a limited definition of place as location.

Fundamentally, Castells's space of flows/places distinction has to do with issues of social difference and power, and in this respect he does share with Massey a general interest in the politics and unevenness of social change. He associates the space of flows with 'dominant processes and functions' (ibid., p. 412) in the network society, while associating the space of places with 'subordinate functions ... and people', who live in physical locales that are, at least in his view, 'increasingly segregated and disconnected from each other' (ibid., p. 476), as well as being disconnected from a space of flows that 'does not permeate down to the whole realm of human experience' (ibid., p. 423). As Castells (ibid., p. 415) expresses the argument at one point: 'The space of power and wealth is projected throughout the world, while people's life and experience is rooted in places ... people are local.' His contention is that, as a result of the increasing divergence of these 'two forms of space', 'we may be heading toward life in parallel universes' (ibid., p. 428).

These claims of Castells's require careful inspection. Once more, on the face of it, he appears to be in line with Massey, because her ideas on the power geometry of time-space compression, as well as her findings on the activity spaces of social groups living in Cambridgeshire villages, indicate a division between powerful people who are 'doing the moving and communicating' and subordinate groups who are more 'rooted' in their physical locations (see also Massey, 1994, p. 148, for some interesting comments on the physically isolated Pacific islanders who have jets flying high above them). However, her account of spatiality and mobility has greater subtlety than his because she realises that 'there are also groups ... doing a lot of physical moving ... who are not in charge of the process in the same way' (ibid., p. 149) as those she calls the jet-setters. Furthermore, Castells's assertion that 'the overwhelming majority of people' live in a space of places that is disconnected from flows or mobilities, and, even more puzzlingly, his claim that the sites within this space of places are 'locales whose ... function and meaning are self-contained within the boundaries of physical contiguity' (Castells, 1996, p. 423), go against the grain of Massey's global-sense-of-place thesis, as well as her rejection of place-as-closed assumptions. His statement that 'people are local' does not appear to acknowledge the transformation of (ordinary) localities in circumstances of globalisation, in which 'nobody in the first world these days lives ... completely locally' (Massey, 1995, p. 60), not even 'the most "local" ... people'. When defining the space of places as 'segregated' and 'self-contained', Castells therefore seems to be forgetting about the mundane experiences of deterritorialisation that are identified by Tomlinson (1999).

Indeed, I would argue that Castells's main example in his discussion of the space of places actually serves to confirm some of the problems with his social theory of space. Just as Massey wrote about Kilburn as a district of London that was familiar to her, so Castells (1996, pp. 423–5) describes a district of Paris named Belleville, where he had lived back in the 1960s. He writes:

> Belleville was, as for so many immigrants throughout its history, my entry point to Paris. ... As a 20-year-old political exile ... I was given shelter by a Spanish construction worker ... who introduced me to ...

the place. … Thirty years after our first encounter … Belleville is still a place. … The new immigrants (Asians, Yugoslavs) have joined a long-established stream of Tunisian Jews, Maghrebian Muslims, and Southern Europeans, themselves the successors of the intra-urban exiles pushed into Belleville in the nineteenth century. … New middle-class households, generally young, have joined the neighbor-hood because of its urban vitality. … Cultures and histories, in a truly plural urbanity, interact in the space.

(ibid., pp. 423–4)

On the evidence of his description in this passage, Belleville is surely far from being 'self-contained within the boundaries of physical contiguity' (ibid., p. 423). I have no difficulty in agreeing with him that it is a distinc-tive location, but all of the factors mentioned in the passage, including the story of his own arrival there from Spain, involve specific links to 'else-where', both across the city of Paris and out across the globe in different directions. Belleville's uniqueness has been formed precisely through a cultural mix or confluence in a particular urban environment, and his example is a good illustration of what Massey terms the openness of places. In addition to these streams of transnational physical migration and 'intra-urban' movement that have helped to shape the character of the district, it would be reasonable to assume that the contemporary residents of Belleville have access to numerous 'flows of information … flows of images … sounds' (ibid., p. 412) in their routine practices of everyday living. Interestingly, as David Bell (2007, p. 74) observes:

In later writing … Castells revises his view … to see the space of flows and the space of places as more coterminous, or folded together – he … also sees an error in his own prior articulation of the space of flows only to the techno-elites.

For instance, rather than seeing the space of flows and the space of places as diametrically opposed spatial forms, leading inevitably 'toward life in parallel universes' (Castells, 1996, p. 428), he subsequently concedes that 'the geography of the new history will not be made, after all, of the separation between places and flows, but out of the interface between places and flows' (Castells, 2000, p. 27; and see Castells, 2005). My strong preference is for this later, revised perspective of Castells's, which I believe fits much better with Massey's view of a global sense of place, and with the more general case that I have been developing in my book (that is, the case for an understanding of various mobilities as pivotal to the constitution of places in social life).

The Social as Mobility

I come next to Urry's work, and especially to *Sociology beyond Societies: Mobilities for the Twenty-first Century* (2000) and *Mobilities* (2007). With these two single-authored books, and with a range of related publications including co-authored articles and books (for example, Hannam *et al.*, 2006; Larsen *et al.*, 2006; Sheller and Urry, 2006; Elliott and Urry, 2010), Urry has done perhaps more than any other theorist over recent years to establish the study of mobilities in the social sciences and humanities (see also Cresswell, 2006; Tomlinson, 2007; Adey, 2010; Cresswell and Merriman, 2011, for a selection of further important books on mobility that have been published in the recent past). Urry's turn to mobilities can be linked to his earlier development of a distinctive sociology of tourism (Urry, 1990), which explored issues to do with the social significance of travel in contemporary living. It is worth noting, too, that his previous writings have included a number of essays on the sociology of place (collected in Urry, 1995). In this section of the chapter, my aim is to outline what I regard as the key aspects of Urry's theory of 'the "social as mobility"' (Urry, 2000, p. 2), and, in concluding my discussion of his work, I will reflect on the ways in which he deals with place and dwelling in relation to travel or mobility.

Earlier in this chapter, I wrote of Appadurai's call for a transnational anthropology (Appadurai, 1996), and *Sociology beyond Societies* (Urry, 2000) might be understood, at least in part, as Urry's call for a transnational sociology. The book's title indicates his wish to 'interrogate the concept of the social as society and show that, whatever its value in the past, it will not in the future be especially relevant as the organising concept of sociological analysis' (ibid., p. 1). His contention is that the idea of 'society', which has been 'central to sociological discourse' (ibid., pp. 5–6), 'is embedded within notions of nation-state ... national society', whereas he describes his book as: 'a manifesto for a sociology that examines the diverse mobilities of peoples, objects, images, information ... the development of various global "networks and flows"' (ibid., p. 1; and notice the similarities here with how Castells, 1996, defines the space of flows). When I say, though, that he is 'in part' calling for a transnational sociology, this is because it is important to see that alongside his concern with global flows, or what Peter Adey (2010, p. 9) calls 'big mobilities', Urry also takes an interest in some of the 'little mobilities' (ibid., p. 6) of everyday living. Indeed, these 'big' and 'little' movements may be closely intertwined. In addition, I should say that while I am sympathetic to his 'manifesto' for a sociology of 'diverse mobilities' and his Massey-like argument that (national) 'borders are porous' (Urry, 2000, p. 18), I do find myself wondering why Urry seems to rule out the possibility of rearticulating the concept of 'the social as society' (since the notion of a 'network society', for instance, is evidently intended by Castells, 1996, to signal transformations on a transnational scale, where flows or mobilities cross national frontiers).

For me, the most crucial feature of Urry's recent sociological analysis is his account of what he refers to as the 'five interdependent "mobilities" that produce social life organized across distance' (Urry, 2007, p. 47; and see Urry, 2000, pp. 49–76, on the first four of these; Elliott and Urry, 2010, pp. 15–16), because this account of various 'travellings' helpfully serves to 'insert communications into the study of travel and transport' (Urry, 2007, p. 157; see also Morley, 2009). I now discuss these 'interdependent "mobilities"'.

To begin with, Urry (2007, pp. 47–8) points to the physical movement or 'corporeal travel' that people are engaged in for the purposes of, for example, 'work, leisure ... migration and escape' (and his use of the word 'corporeal' emphasises the involvement of bodies in this movement):

> Such bodies encounter ... the physical world ... sensuously. ... The body ... senses as it moves. ... Especially important in that sense of movement ... is ... touch, of the feet on the pavement or the ... path, the hands on ... the steering wheel. Various ... technologies facilitate this ... sense as they ... extend human capacities.

I have chosen to quote this particular passage because it clearly demonstrates the connections that *Mobilities* has with the phenomenological perspectives discussed in detail in the previous chapter. For instance, I hear echoes of Nigel Thrift's non-representational theory, Tim Ingold's dwelling perspective and Maurice Merleau-Ponty's philosophy of embodiment (in Urry's references here to the sensuousness of practice, the mobilities of walking/driving, the significance of touch, and the technological extension of bodies and the senses to constitute what he calls 'hybrid assemblages ... of humans, objects, technologies', see Urry, 2007, p. 48). To the concerns with walking and driving that he shares with other theorists cited earlier in my book, Urry (ibid., pp. 135–56) adds a strong commitment to the study of what he and some colleagues have termed the 'aeromobilities' (Cwerner et al., 2009) of passengering by plane.

Meanwhile, closely related to the corporeal travel of people, there is a second type of mobility: 'The physical movement of objects' (Urry,

2007, p. 47; on the 'social lives' of 'things-in-motion', see also Appadurai, 1986). Examples of such things-in-motion, for Urry (2000, p. 65), include the 'souvenirs' that travel home with tourists who have purchased them on foreign holidays, which come to rest on 'the mantelpiece' or 'sideboard', but also a portable technology like the Walkman (and I will be discussing other mobile media shortly), which moves around with its user as what Merleau-Ponty (2002 [1962], p. 176) might call 'a bodily auxiliary'. A further example, which helps to illustrate Tomlinson's point about what global modernity brings to people in their local settings, would be the remarkable transnational movements of foodstuffs that come to appear, in a typically unremarkable, taken-for-granted fashion, on the shelves of supermarkets, to be carried home by shoppers. Incidentally, the case of the supermarket, with its global network of food supply and its local practices of shopping, is a specific instance in which big mobilities and little mobilities (Adey, 2010) are closely intertwined.

The three other sorts of mobility identified by Urry (2007), starting with imaginative travel, are all afforded by the uses of media of communication. He associates imaginative travelling primarily with practices of television viewing, although he acknowledges, too, that 'people "travel" elsewhere through ... guidebooks and brochures, travel writing, photos, postcards, radio and film' (ibid., p. 169). Interestingly, with reference to Paddy Scannell's phenomenological approach to broadcasting (Scannell, 1996), Urry (2000, pp. 67–9) observes that watching a live event on television 'enables one to be ... in two places at once':

> We imaginatively travel and are at Princess Diana's funeral ... seeing the world record being broken ... and so on. ... People are thrown into the public world disclosed ... on television ... and ... distant events, personalities and happenings are mundanely brought into the living room.

In my own earlier work (as far back as Moores, 1993b), I have commented on the ways in which television viewing 'simultaneously combines "staying home" and, via electronically mediated sounds and images, "going places"' (Moores, 2000, p. 96), and there are a few other instances in which contemporary media theorists have conceptualised television as a technology of travel or 'a means of transport' (see especially Larsen, 1999; Morley, 2000, 2010). An important qualification I want to make at this stage, though, is that the notion of travelling 'imaginatively' must not divert attention away from the profoundly embodied and sensuous character of media use (indeed, see Urry, 2000, pp. 89–90, on the human senses, including hearing, involved in acts of 'watching' television). As I argued in the previous chapter with reference to practices of pointing and pressing or clicking, it is necessary to appreciate how bodily knowledge and experience are linked directly with technologically mediated mobilities, and to consider physical and media environments jointly as lived or inhabited spaces. The same point applies, of course, to what Urry (ibid., p. 70; see also Urry, 2007, p. 159) names 'virtual travel' via networked computers, and it is to this form of mobility that I turn next.

In a piece on matters of mobility and proximity, which was published in the period between *Sociology beyond Societies* and *Mobilities*, Urry (2002, pp. 265–7) proposes that the virtual travel of internet communications has given rise to a 'virtual proximity': 'The kinds of travel and presencing involved ... change the character and experience of "co-presence", since people can feel proximate while ... distant.' I am inclined to regard this virtual, computer-mediated proximity less in terms of 'change' and more in terms of continuity with another sort of electronically mediated presencing (Scannell, 1996, p. 84) or intimacy at a distance (Horton and Wohl, 1956; Meyrowitz, 1985, pp. 119–21; Thompson, 1995, pp. 219–25), which is linked to what Urry terms the imaginative travel of television viewing. In the same piece (Urry, 2002), though, he makes a further proposal that I take to be of greater significance. He insists that virtual travel and virtual proximity do not straightforwardly 'substitute' for physical movement and physical co-presence.

Drawing on the work of Deirdre Boden and Harvey Molotch (1994) on 'the compulsion of proximity' (that is, physical proximity), Urry (2002, p. 256) asks 'a very simple question: why do people physically travel?' In an age of imaginative and virtual mobilities, then, why still bother with the corporeal travel that is required in order to be 'face-to-face, face-the-place and face-the-moment' (ibid., pp. 261–2), with other people who are usually physically absent, with particular locations that 'need to be seen "for oneself"' and with particular events that 'cannot be "missed"'? For specific individuals and social groups, the answers may be clear enough (Urry understands such answers to be bound up with various experiences of 'obligation'), but these questions should not imply any universal judgement that the physically proximate is always preferable to the imaginatively or virtually proximate. In fact, people sometimes prefer an intimacy at a distance to a bodily being there (and even Boden and Molotch, 1994, p. 260, acknowledge that, occasionally, physical co-presence 'is "not enough" ... conventional etiquette places a premium on a written "thank you" for a nice dinner, rather than only the "too easy" face-to-face version delivered when taking one's leave'). Urry's principal argument, emerging out of his consideration of such issues, is that an investigation of the overlapping of different types of travelling and communicating is vital, hence his overall perspective on mobilities as 'interdependent' (Urry, 2007, p. 47). For instance, in *Sociology beyond Societies* he was already realising that 'virtual travel has to be understood in relation to corporeal travel' (Urry, 2000, p. 75; see again Kendall, 2002, on how some inhabitants of a virtual pub physically travel to attend 'offline gatherings'), and, more generally, that there are 'complex interrelations between the flows of electronic messages and of people' (echoing Appadurai, 1996, on the connections between mediascapes and ethnoscapes).

Urry's fifth form of mobility is 'mobile communicative travel' (2007, p. 171), and this final category in his list of mobilities best exemplifies the 'complex interrelations' between communications and transport, since it refers to the increasing number of media technologies, including the 'iPod ... laptop computer ... and ... mobile phone', which have been explicitly designed for people to use while on the move, in contexts of corporeal travel (although he offers a reminder, too, that older media like the 'book, magazine and newspaper ... were also portable'). With regard to the embodied character of media use, it is interesting to note that some of the latest mobile communication devices are operated by touching and moving fingers across the screen itself, as a way of manipulating and navigating media spaces. There are two of Urry's observations on mobile communicative travel that I want to highlight briefly, both of which can be illustrated with material from recent empirical research projects (Larsen *et al.*, 2006; Elliott and Urry, 2010).

One of these observations has to do with the formation of what Urry (2007, p. 173) names 'fluid meeting cultures'. His point is that the potential for mobile phoning and texting while physically dispersed or travelling in public settings has led to circumstances in which the 'clock-time of ... wrist watches is ... supplemented by a ... fluid time of mobile communications ... coordination was once finalized before departure ... it is now often negotiated and performed on the move' (ibid.; and see again Ling, 2004, pp. 73–6, on a contemporary 'softening' of schedules). This fluidity is audible in the following extract from an interview (see Larsen *et al.*, 2006, p. 120), in which a young woman from Manchester explains how she negotiates an evening out for a drink with her friends:

'It's usually a loose arrangement, say meet up roughly 8 o'clock ... but most of the time that changes ... you've got mobiles, you can do that ... I'm running late or we ... go to a different bar.'

Another, rather different observation on mobile communicative travel, which Urry makes with fellow sociologist and co-author Anthony Elliott (Elliott and Urry, 2010, p. 6), concerns 'affect storage and retrieval'. Their collaborative work shows a special interest in questions of 'lived experience' (ibid., p. xi), and they refer at several moments in their book to 'narratives drawn from in-depth interviews conducted with people ... navigating ... mobile worlds'. For example, in the opening story of a Brazilian-born academic based in London, whose 'hurried (and harried) professional life transports her through various major cities of the planet' (ibid., p. 2), there is the following account of her experience in a cafe in New York:

> Sitting down to coffee and launching her Apple laptop, she scans through the academic paper she will read tomorrow at the conference. Unable to concentrate, she picks up the phone and dials London, hoping to reach her husband and above all to talk with her daughter before ... bed. But she has not brought the correct adapter to recharge the battery of her mobile. Frustrated ... she ... is able to activate iTunes on her laptop and selects a song that vividly evokes emotions she feels for her family.

Commenting on her choice and use of a song with which she is thoroughly familiar and emotionally caught up, the authors acknowledge that people have often ' "used" music to evoke memory' (ibid.) in the past, and yet the arrival of new mobile audio (and visual) technologies 'alters the social contexts in which people can access music' (as well as digital photography and film, see ibid., p. 27). They argue, then, that such media 'enable people to deposit ... moods and dispositions ... until they are "withdrawn" ' (ibid., p. 6). Although I have some difficulty with the assertion that it is emotion that gets stored in technology (partly because the notion that feelings are deposited and 'withdrawn' suggests a rather rational banking activity), this attention to affect does serve, once again, to connect Urry's ideas on the social as mobility with non-representational theory. The story of this woman's listening practice also reminds me very much of Tuan's remarks on returning to a favourite musical piece 'to be in the midst of a magical place' (Tuan, 2004, p. 53), indicating a link with phenomenological geography too.

Let me complete this section now by reflecting on how Urry's work on mobilities deals with place and dwelling. In my outline of that work so far, I hope to have shown not only that he has a sophisticated understanding of the social as mobility but also that his analysis has the potential to relate practices of dwelling and travelling (see Clifford, 1997) in interesting ways. This potential is indicated, in particular, by Urry's references to the corporeal and the emotional, and to 'hybrid assemblages' (Urry, 2007, p. 48) of humans and technologies. These specific dimensions of his work point precisely to issues of habit, affect and attachment to environment in everyday living (while promising to widen those perspectives discussed in my previous chapter, by taking greater account of 'large-scale movements ... across the world, as well as ... more local processes', see Hannam *et al.*, 2006, p. 1). In my view, however, the potential is never quite fulfilled in Urry's *Mobilities*, despite the fact that a whole chapter is devoted to a discussion of places (Urry, 2007, pp. 253–70). This part of his book builds on the background that he has in the sociology of tourism, and it contains some fascinating material on extraordinary 'places of attraction' (ibid., p. 253) and on 'competition between places ... as they struggle for positioning on a global stage' (ibid., p. 269). Yet I believe that he misses an opportunity here, by not exploring the ordinary accomplishment of place through routine activities of dwelling ('in a world of flux', see Morley, 2000, p. 13).

Elsewhere in *Mobilities*, Urry (2007, pp. 124–30) does cite Heidegger (1993 [1971]) before providing a valuable discussion of 'inhabiting cars' (see again Bull, 2001, 2007; Thrift, 2004a, 2007), but it is necessary to return to *Sociology beyond Societies* for a more detailed consideration of 'dwellings' in relation to travellings (Urry, 2000, pp. 131–60). At one point there, Urry (ibid., p. 140) offers a view of place as 'multiplex' and as a 'particular nexus', in a manner that recalls Massey's perspective on the multiple identities of localities and on place as an intersection of local and global social relations:

> Places can be loosely understood ... as multiplex, as a set of spaces where ... networks and flows coalesce. ... Any such place can be viewed as the particular nexus between ... propinquity characterised by intensely thick co-present interaction, and ... fast flowing ... networks stretched ... across distances. These propinquities and extensive networks come together to enable performances in, and of, particular places.

Crucially, the notion of 'performances ... of ... places', mentioned at the end of this extract, also reminds me of Seamon's idea of place choreographies (Seamon, 1979, pp. 54–6), although Urry sees how these performances incorporate 'extensive networks' as well as 'propinquities', in a way that Seamon and his fellow phenomenological geographers do not, or else only acknowledge implicitly. Whereas Seamon (ibid., p. 91) has a tendency to regard 'mobility and mass communications' as a threat to place-making, Urry (2000, p. 132) argues that: 'contemporary forms of dwelling almost always involve diverse forms of mobility' (including those imaginative, virtual and mobile communicative travellings that are associated with technologically mediated interaction).

I Know How to Get Around

I draw the chapter to a close in this section by reporting on a collaborative research project that I was involved in recently (see also Moores and Metykova, 2009, 2010). At this point in the book, I turn to that qualitative empirical research, which was on the environmental experiences of trans-European migrants, because it provides me with an opportunity to strengthen the connection I have just made between Urry's interests in 'diverse forms of mobility' (Urry, 2000, p. 132) and the work done by Seamon and others in phenomenological geography. As I emphasised in the previous chapter, these geographers are associated with the development of a helpful conceptualisation of place as a practical and emotional accomplishment.

Following a significant expansion of the European Union in 2004, many young people from the new member states in Eastern Europe moved to live and work in the UK. By late 2007, according to official statistics from the UK government's worker-registration scheme, close to 800,000 migrants from those countries had come to the UK (it is likely that the statistics underestimate the actual number), with the vast majority in the 18–34 age range. During that period, there was much public discussion in Britain about the number of people arriving from Eastern Europe, with the debate being centred, rather predictably, on the consequences of these transnational migrations for the UK's regional or national economies and cultures. In this particular political context, the project was designed to pay serious attention to the experiences of some of the migrants themselves (focusing specifically on issues of environmental experience, see Tuan, 1977, p. v; Seamon, 1979, p. 15), including their experiences of media environments (Meyrowitz, 1985).

Before I offer examples of the material that emerged from the research, it is important for me to say something about the project's methodological approach. There is a problem facing any researchers who are setting out to investigate issues of environmental experience, and this problem has to do with the division between practical and discursive knowledge (Crossley, 2001, p. 122) that was referred to earlier in my book. If the inhabiting of everyday physical and media environments involves a practical, bodily know-how (a knowing how to get around), research participants may have difficulty in bringing aspects of that pre-reflective knowing to what Anthony Giddens (1984, p. 7) terms 'discursive consciousness' (and yet it is worth noting that Giddens does not regard the distinction between the practical and the discursive as 'a rigid and impermeable one'). In other words, if place is accomplished through repetitive, habitual practices and is usually taken for granted, then it is likely to be hard to get people to talk at length about place-making. One possible solution to the problem would be to use what Urry (2007, pp. 39–40) calls mobile methods of research, 'travelling with people' as they get around and observing their routine activities. However, in the collaborative research project being discussed here, Monika Metykova and I decided to persist with the technique of in-depth conversational interviewing that has long been employed in qualitative empirical research. In order to appreciate our reason for doing so, it is necessary to return to a point that I made in my commentary on Seamon's *A Geography of the Lifeworld* (1979). There, I wrote of how members of his environmental-experience groups found that they were able to reflect on certain everyday movements and affective attachments following occasional, minor disruptions of routine. So when basic contact with familiar environments got disturbed, it gave rise to a noticing of what is typically unnoticed. Might it be, then, that transnational physical migrations often result in more profound and prolonged disruptions of routine? Could these be social circumstances in which people are able to bring aspects of practical knowledge to discursive consciousness ('to articulate what was previously just lived out', see Taylor, 2005, p. 32)? Furthermore, might an investigation of that period following the event of migration be one in which researchers have a chance to understand how people reconstitute their senses of place, as they re-establish familiarity through ordered patterns of movement (see also Seamon, 1989, for his own discussion of migrant experiences, based on an analysis of literary fictions, and for his account of a process that he names 'the dwelling-journey spiral')?

Two other preliminary points need to be made at this stage. First, although I am posing general questions about the relationship between transnational migrations and senses of place (suggesting that migration provides an opportunity to explore performances of places), there is, of course, no singular, universally shared experience of migration, just as there is no singular, universally shared lifeworld that gets disturbed. There are historically and culturally specific conditions of migration, and these conditions matter for migrant experiences. For example, whereas most people migrating on a ship from Europe to North America in the 1800s were making 'a journey which breaks them loose irrevocably from their former sphere of dwelling' (ibid., p. 232), the break for contemporary trans-European migrants is not an irrevocable one. Many cities in Eastern Europe can be reached from Britain by plane in only a few hours, since there are regular flights to these destinations, many of which are on routes operated by budget airlines. This means that there is the potential for migrants to take trips back to, and to receive visitors from, the countries from which they came. Indeed, there is the ongoing potential for 'return migration'. Friends and family members in those countries and elsewhere are also reachable via internet and phone services, by means of virtual and mobile communicative travel (Urry, 2007). Second, and more briefly, it may be that access to familiar media environments is especially significant for some transnational migrants today, given their largely unfamiliar material surroundings soon after arriving in a new physical location. While much has been written on media, migration and diaspora (for instance, see the collections edited by King and Wood, 2001; Karim, 2003; Bailey *et al.*, 2007), there is still very little research that concentrates, as this project did, on the period following the event of migration (but see the valuable work carried out by O'Neill, 2007, with asylum seekers and refugees in the UK).

Conversational interviews with twenty young people, all within the 18–34 age range, who had migrated to the UK following the European Union's expansion in 2004, were recorded and transcribed by my co-researcher during 2006 and 2007. At the time of the interviews, these young people were based in London, Newcastle or Edinburgh. The interviews were held in cafe, bar or household settings and their average length was over one and a half hours. Some of the interviews were conducted in Hungarian, Czech or Slovakian and translated into English, while others were conducted in English.

As a way of opening up my discussion of key themes running through the empirical data, I now offer a few fragments of material that come from an interview with a Hungarian woman called Petra. When the interview was recorded in early 2007, she had been living in London for a year and a half, having moved there from Budapest, and she was working as a nanny. Petra spoke of how, initially, she had found living in London to be strange and alienating. There were several reasons for this experience of existential outsideness (Relph, 2008 [1976], p. 51) on arrival, from her continually looking in the wrong direction as she stepped off the pavement to cross the road ('once I was almost run over') to being treated 'with disdain' by her first employer. After a year and a half, though, she talked about her growing familiarity with those parts of the city that she frequented on foot and on public transport, and, in relation to her patterns of movement and her knowing how to get around (what Taylor, 2005, p. 34, terms 'navigational know-how'), she was also able to reflect on an emerging affective attachment to the urban environment:

> It's no longer like 'Oh my God, I want to go from here to here. How do I do that?' I know how to do that. I know how to get around. ... It was really nice because my parents visited me ... nice that I could show them this and that. I travelled with them on the underground and my dad told me he was so proud that I could cope in this huge city, that he would be lost. ... It's such a good feeling. ... There were difficult times at the beginning, but now ... it's good. ... To some extent, I consider myself a Londoner.

Alongside that growing familiarity with, and feeling for, her new city, Petra was becoming increasingly aware of her already established affective attachment to Budapest. Indeed, this attachment was brought to her attention by her physical absence from the city that she used to live in. She told the following story about going to book a flight, 'in the Malev Airlines office' in London, for a trip back to Hungary: 'The office is full of photos of Budapest, and there was an English guy telling me to come and have nostalgic moments over the pictures any time.' The images on display allowed her to travel imaginatively (Urry, 2000, 2007), and, more generally, media of communication helped her to maintain contact with people and happenings in Hungary. For instance, she spoke of making routine phone calls to a friend in Budapest, and commented that she and her two Hungarian flatmates in London would regularly 'check the net for home news', adding that: 'We are always at home in home news' (it is interesting to juxtapose the at-homeness of these recent migrants in 'home news' with the conclusions reached by Aksoy and Robins, 2003, p. 103, who, in their study of the television viewing practices of long-time 'London Turks', remark on how the 'conditions no longer exist for feeling at home' in Turkish news programmes watched live via satellite).

The first of four themes suggested by this account of Petra's environmental experiences is that of trans-European migrants' initial impressions on arrival in Britain. Not all of the interviewees shared her experience of existential outsideness. Notable exceptions were those few who had spent periods living and working abroad before. For instance, soon after arriving in London, a Czech woman named Katerina, who had been an au pair there several years earlier, enjoyed visiting 'favourite places' she could remember from that previous stay. However, there are many stories of initial strangeness and alienation in the interview material. Let me give just a couple of examples here.

There is the case of Simona, a Lithuanian woman from Vilnius who came to live in London. Although she had grown up in the Lithuanian capital, and made the journey to London fully expecting to find a city much larger than Vilnius, she was still overwhelmed by the scale and pace of urban living in the English capital: 'My first impression was "it's huge" ... something more than I expected ... the huge amount of people ... so busy ... I couldn't grasp it ... it was like ... "Oh my God, can I stay here?"' A further example is the case of Agnes, a Hungarian woman who, like Petra, had left Budapest. For Agnes, the move to the UK was to Newcastle, where she was employed by a large computer company based on the outskirts of the city, commuting to work by car. She explained that:

> I was driving from the very beginning ... driving on the other side, sitting in the car on the other side. I didn't know where I was, a big challenge. ... For a long time, when I knew I'd have to drive somewhere, I had a stomach ache ... studying the map for half an hour and then, once I arrived, half an hour of catching my breath.

Just as Petra, as a pedestrian, had trouble with the way in which 'you had to look in a different direction when you stepped off the pavement', so Agnes was initially uncomfortable about 'driving on the other side' of the road and being seated at the wheel in a different location. Her embodied discomfort, which is evident here in the references to stomach aches and 'catching my breath', had precisely to do with a lack of familiarity (a not knowing how to get around) in the new spaces of the car and the urban scene. Merleau-Ponty (2002 [1962], p. 165) writes of 'the habit of driving a car', and that habitual practice is temporarily disrupted when there are major changes in the driver's environmental conditions.

A second theme running through the empirical data is the gradual emergence of senses of place in new physical surroundings. Petra developed a growing familiarity with, and feeling for, the parts of London that she frequented on foot and on public transport, learning how to find her way about there. In Tuan's terms, 'what was strange town' (Tuan, 1977, p. 199) became 'familiar place'. Petra's place-making involved some of the 'movements in the outdoor environment' that Seamon (1979, p. 33) identifies as an important part of people's time-space routines, and there are numerous examples in the interview material of how such corporeal mobilities (including habits of walking, driving, travelling by bus and by train) facilitated at-homeness.

For instance, returning to the interview with Agnes, the young woman who had struggled with driving a car around Newcastle, it is interesting that she went on to reveal how her fear of driving there 'disappeared ... after about half a year'. 'I became a routine driver', she explained, 'discovering the city in small steps.' Similarly, a Slovakian man named Boris, who was employed as a van driver delivering food for a catering company in inner London, commented that: 'if you work in one area for two years then you find your way, even blindfolded'. Meanwhile, for Marcin, a Polish man working as a 'domestic' in an Edinburgh hospital, repetitive practices of walking and travelling by bus were contributing to the formation of a sense of place:

> On my way to work every day, I meet the same people, just knowing each other by sight. The lady goes the same time in the same direction. It's amazing that we're catching the bus in exactly the same place.

What he pointed to, then, was a meshing of morning routines in the public setting of an urban street (one element of a far larger collaborative 'dance' of bodies and things in the city, see Seamon, 1979; Thrift, 2009).

In addition, certain movements (and also moments of stillness or rest) in indoor environments were important for the creation of at-homeness in everyday living. Two brief examples of this can be heard in an interview with Ilija, a Slovenian man from Ljubljana, who was employed as a researcher in a university science department in London. He talked about feeling comfortable in the old library building at his university, remarking on its 'special smell' and on the floorboards that were 'squeaky' underfoot. In the private setting of his rented apartment, too, Ilija was, in his own words, 'at home ... in the bathroom' in particular, where he had got into the habit of taking 'a long bath' at the end of each day, initially because the shower was broken.

The third theme opened up by my earlier account of Petra's experiences is reflections on previously taken-for-granted, established senses of place. Immersion in everyday environments and the unselfconscious feeling of 'belonging' that Relph (2008 [1976], p. 55) calls existential insideness are especially difficult to investigate empirically, yet most of the interviewees were able to speak about aspects of the lifeworlds they had known, practically and emotionally, prior to their migrations. As I have stated, a fundamental feature of the collaborative research project that I am reporting on here was its interest in whether transnational physical migration might result in a significant disruption of routines, which would then allow room for reflection on the pre-reflective or for remarking on what once seemed to be unremarkable because it was formerly 'just lived out' (Taylor, 2005, p. 32).

For Simona, the young woman from Lithuania who had moved to and eventually settled in London, it was occasional trips back to Vilnius that focused her reflections on what had previously been taken for granted:

> When I go back there I really feel like at home, you know, walking the streets of Vilnius. ... Yeah, it's different because I no longer live there, but it still feels like home ... you feel it's your own town ... because so many things happened there ... for me. ... I walk there, this happened there, there it was that, the atmosphere ... the mood ... these streets carry meaning. ... I never realised that before I left, I didn't realise how attached I am.

A very similar example can be found in an interview with Honza, a Czech man living and working in London. He described going back to visit the city where he had grown up: 'When I arrive in Hradec, I simply know every corner, every street and every pub ... I walk ... I'm at home.'

Another case of someone who noticed a formerly unnoticed 'insideness' is that of Darek, a Polish man employed as a cleaner in Edinburgh. He declares:

> I love our culture in Poland ... now, when I live here, I see that. ... When you have something every day you don't appreciate it, but when you have it only a few times, when you move to another country and you don't have contact with it like before, you ... miss it.

Still, it is important to note that a few of the interviewees experienced a loosening of their emotional ties with former locations in Eastern Europe. For instance, Magda, a Polish woman living in Edinburgh, where she was a care worker with the elderly, talked in the following way about her emotions when making a return visit to Poland: 'I feel like I belonged ... before, but I don't belong ... now ... after a couple of days I feel like I want to be back here' (that is, in Scotland).

Closely connected with these migrants' experiences of occasional return visits, a fourth and final theme is the reach (Buttimer, 1980) that is afforded by trans-European transport and communication links (and the associated transnational mobilities of 'peoples, objects, images, information', see Urry, 2000, p. 1). In thinking about the distinctive characteristics of contemporary trans-European migration, it is necessary to take account of the relative physical nearness of Britain and Eastern Europe, in comparison with the distances involved in travelling between, say, Europe and North America or South Asia. Of course, moving across a continent is a major relocation, but, as I indicated earlier, many cities in Eastern Europe are only a few hours away by plane. In addition, as discussed in my opening chapter, the uses of electronic media have changed the geography of proximal experience, serving to double reality instantaneously (Scannell, 1996). Of particular interest in this regard is the potential for media environments, which overlay physical settings, to be significant places for migrants who return to them again and again (Tuan, 2004), as Petra and her flatmates returned to Hungarian news sites on the internet.

Consider the case of Krzysztof, a Polish man from Wroclaw who was living in London. He said that: 'Gatwick Airport is very convenient and ... from the time I leave ... to the time I enter my mother's house it takes about five hours.' However, he was not only travelling back to Wroclaw by plane. Krzysztof also maintained a familiarity of a sort with that city (a virtual proximity, see Urry, 2002) by regularly engaging in virtual travel. For 'at least half an hour a day', he looked at a website that displayed digital photographs of buildings in Wroclaw as it was going through a period of urban regeneration. As he explained: 'People take pictures and put them on the website, and ... I actually know more about what's going on in the city than my mum.' His inhabiting of that online environment resembled Petra's routine checking of home news, and there are several other stories in the interview material of migrants using the internet in this way. For example, a Slovakian man named Julius, who was working in London as a computer programmer, told how he watched webcam images of the River Danube while sitting at his desk during coffee breaks in the office.

More generally, the uses of communication technologies were typically woven into everyday routines. For instance, in the case of Agnes, online contact with her mother in Hungary was maintained while at work in Newcastle: 'She's got email at work too, so we exchange emails during the day and phone each other from time to time.' Meanwhile, for Marcin in Edinburgh, 'coming home from the job' each working day was associated with the ritual of checking his email inbox for any new messages from Poland: 'I try to be in touch regularly with my family.' When he occasionally made physical journeys back to Poland from Scotland, he took objects with him to give as small gifts ('shortbread and whisky ... for my family and friends'), and there are many examples in the interview material of the two-way transnational mobilities of objects. So when Boris's girlfriend came to visit him in London, she brought Slovakian biscuits and 'loads and loads of sausages' to make goulash 'with the smell of your homeland'. Moving in the opposite direction, Marius, a Lithuanian man living and working in London, would ferry other people's heavy parcels and luggage back to the city of Kaunas in his car, preferring to travel on the ground rather than in the air.

Relating to this fourth and final theme, I want to make one last point here. Those technologically mediated links with Eastern Europe, to which I have just referred, could sometimes be accompanied by a disconnection from British television news and popular entertainment programmes. Indeed, a majority of the participants in the project did not possess a television set, preferring media with a greater capacity for mediated interpersonal communication, and often a greater portability (for them, television was no longer what Silverstone, 1991, has called the 'leading object' in a range of communication technologies). For example, Simona had little interest in engaging with broadcast news about the city that she was living in: 'My parents call me ... and tell me what's going on in London, actually.' Similarly, Zsuzsanna, a Hungarian woman living in London, spoke of her exclusion from an everyday conversation about a popular 'reality TV' show: 'I didn't know what it was about so I asked ... and everyone stared at me ... as if I lived on another planet ... really embarrassing.' Julius had also found himself excluded from conversations about television between colleagues in his office, explaining that people 'would talk ... about a programme, and ... you are completely left out because ... you're not following it'. In his case, this uncomfortable feeling of being 'left out' eventually led him to buy a tuner card so that he could access live broadcasting via his laptop.

Conclusion: Non-media-centric Media Studies

With a view to developing an original and productive synthesis of ideas on media, place and mobility, I have offered a detailed critical engagement with different areas of academic literature. Looking back at the arguments that I have advanced in this book, I am now in a position to give an overall summary of my key concerns. I am also in a position to make explicit what has been largely implicit in my discussion so far, which is the non-media-centric approach that I am advocating for media studies. On the face of it, the notion of 'non-media-centric media studies' would appear to be a contradiction in terms, but I want to propose that such an approach can provide a valuable way forward for the field of media studies in future years.

I began my critical review with a consideration of Joshua Meyrowitz's second-generation medium theory (Meyrowitz, 1985, 1994), since his work is probably still the best-known attempt to explore relations between media and place (and also because he hints at the importance of technologically mediated mobility). As I emphasised in my commentary on his classic book, *No Sense of Place* (1985), I am sympathetic to his case for studying a transformation in the situational geography of social life. What he opens up there is the possibility of understanding people's dual locations in physical and media environments, and I pursued this point with reference to Paddy Scannell's phenomenology of radio and television (Scannell, 1995, 1996). In particular, I argued that Scannell's doubling-of-place idea is helpful for coming to terms with the organisation of social situations in contemporary society. Indeed, it is preferable to Meyrowitz's no-sense-of-place thesis, for which I have much less sympathy and to which I will be returning in due course. By discussing examples of doubling or pluralisation in the uses of telephones and computers, I showed, too, how the applications of Scannell's concept are by no means limited to the analysis of broadcasting.

Next, in the second and longest chapter of my book, which I regard as pivotal, I took the discussion a stage further. Having touched briefly on phenomenology in the first chapter, in my account of Scannell's *Radio, Television and Modern Life* (1996), I proceeded to pay greater attention to phenomenological philosophy (most notably to Merleau-Ponty, 2002 [1962]), and to a number of phenomenologically inspired approaches in the social sciences and humanities. Crucially, I started that chapter by turning to a definition of place as an experiential accomplishment, as something more than just a location or even a social position (Tuan, 1977). In other words, I went beyond an interest in the mere occupation of spaces, including media spaces, to adopt a wider concern with matters of dwelling or habitation in environments of different sorts. For Tuan (ibid.), then, place gets constituted when space feels thoroughly familiar. It is location that is made meaningful through repetitive, habitual practices. Tuan's focus, like that of fellow phenomenological geographer David Seamon (1979), was on issues of environmental experience, and, in some of his later work (Tuan, 2004), he goes on to reflect on people's affective attachments to media spaces or environments that become places as they are returned to again and again. However, neither Tuan nor Seamon, in his *A Geography of the Lifeworld* (1979), ultimately carry the investigation of everyday media uses as far as they could, hence my efforts to push their experiential perspective on formations of place in precisely that direction.

In that pivotal chapter, I also pointed to the relevance for media studies (and, more generally, for cultural studies) of contemporary approaches that challenge an overemphasis on the cognitive and representational dimensions of social life. For instance, in Nigel Thrift's books, *Spatial Formations* (1996) and *Non-representational Theory: Space/Politics/Affect* (2007), and especially in Tim Ingold's *The Perception of the Environment* (2000) and *Lines: A Brief History* (2007), there are important concerns with practical, embodied and sensuous ways of knowing the world and with what Ingold (ibid.) refers to as the alongly integrated character of inhabitant knowledge. Ingold's consideration of walking as a practice is particularly significant here, because he relates place-making directly to ambulatory movements to, from and around physical locations (and see Lee and Ingold, 2006), connecting matters of place with those of mobility. While I have suggested that these approaches are not quite as novel as they might initially seem to be, since they actually arrive at many of the same conclusions as those reached by the phenomenological geographers in the 1970s (notably Seamon, 1979), I believe that the work of Thrift and Ingold can contribute to a necessary revision of the terms of media analysis. For instance, it is my contention that media theorists and researchers must now attend more closely than they have done previously to issues of embodiment in media use, and to what Maurice Merleau-Ponty (2002 [1962]), in his *Phenomenology of Perception*, names the acquisition of habit, involving the incorporation of objects by a body-subject. I am proposing, too, that it would be helpful to understand users' engagements with what have been termed media representations or texts, at least partly, as pre-reflective acts of getting around in media settings or environments. The basis for this shift of emphasis is already there in Scannell (1996), when he writes of finding ways about in broadcasting's programme output, but I have built on his foundation by engaging with non-representational theory in the widest sense of that term. What I am calling for, then, is an acknowledgement of the primacy of practices (Thrift, 1999) and a focus on the agent-in-its-environment (Ingold, 2000), so as to break with any lingering, unreconstructed structuralism that is still evident in certain aspects of media studies today.

Of course, I am well aware that there are many academics in my field who will make sense of the direction I am taking as a retreat from questions of social difference and power, and yet, as I have argued with reference to Pierre Bourdieu's sociology of practice (especially Bourdieu, 1990, 2000) and to what has been called corporeal feminism (Grosz, 1994), it need not be. In media studies, such questions have tended to be posed in terms of the politics of symbolic representation and cognitive interpretation, or else they have been about the political economy of media industries, but I want to insist that, important as these are, they are not the only kinds of political question that should be of concern to the field. There is also a politics of bodily knowledge and experience. This has to do, for example, with the ways in which embodied dispositions are intimately caught up in the social divisions and inequalities of class and gender, and I have argued that this body politics (Hass, 2008) has consequences for how the uses or non-uses of media technologies are approached. In addition, linked questions can be raised when considering formations of at-homeness in physical and media environments, in part because collaborative place-making practices are about exclusions as well as inclusions, as demonstrated clearly by Lori Kendall's ethnographic study, *Hanging Out in the Virtual Pub* (2002).

A theme that resurfaced towards the end of my second chapter was that of placelessness. In the decades before and after Meyrowitz (1985) advanced his no-sense-of-place thesis in media studies, similar ideas were put forward in the disciplines of geography (Relph, 2008 [1976]) and anthropology (Augé, 2009 [1995]). What runs through these ideas about placelessness and non-places is a problematic assumption that developments in media and transportation have weakened senses of place, and that the spaces of so-called mass communication are somehow innately placeless and anonymous. Mobility therefore tends to be seen by Edward Relph (2008 [1976]) and Marc Augé (2009 [1995]) as an obstacle to place-making, whereas I have argued that mobilities of various types, including those that are technologically mediated, are significant for the constitution of places in social life. Even major international airports can have their distinctive place choreographies, as illustrated by Tim Cresswell in *On the Move: Mobility in the Modern Western World* (2006). Indeed, Meyrowitz (2005) seems to have begun to shift towards such a position, with his acknowledgement that electronically mediated communications may enhance attachment to physical environments as communities of interaction become more mobile.

In my third chapter, I continued to explore the relations between place and mobility, but with an emphasis on transnational mobilities and their consequences for what David Morley (2000) calls forms of dwelling in a world of flux. Following James Clifford's lead (Clifford, 1992, 1997), I entered into a joint consideration of practices of dwelling and travelling in circumstances of globalisation, taking the discussion a stage further still. One of the undoubted strengths of the perspectives that I discussed there is a refusal to understand places as bounded entities in any straightforward way. For example, in Doreen Massey's book, *World City* (2007), she points to the difficulty of drawing lines around a metropolis like London, with its vast geography of relations that spread out across the earth, and her earlier work on a global sense of place had already stressed the openness or permeability of her own local district of that city (Massey, 1991, 1994). An additional strength of Massey's perspective, in my view, is the attention that she gives to political questions about place and mobility, most notably through the application of her concept of the power geometry of time-space compression. With differing degrees of success, other social theorists, such as Manuel Castells in *The Rise of the Network Society* (1996) and John Urry in *Sociology beyond Societies* (2000), raise similar issues that have to do with the intersection of local and global social relations (and I showed how Urry, 2007, offers an important contribution to media analysis with his notions of imaginative, virtual and mobile communicative travellings). By reflecting on the significance of extensive networks and flows (as well as physically co-present interactions) for performances of places, Urry (2000), like Massey (1994) before him, is able to deal with an element of place-making that was not explicitly addressed in Tuan's

Space and Place (1977) or in Seamon's innovative lifeworld research (Seamon, 1979). However, ultimately in the third chapter, I returned to the concerns that the phenomenological geographers have with the details of everyday environmental experience, while looking to link their interests in dwelling or habitation rather more directly with the range of interdependent mobilities identified by Urry.

The empirical research project that I reported on in the final section of the third chapter was an investigation into the experiences of some contemporary trans-European migrants. Its approach involved concentrating on the period soon after the event of physical migration and, in addition, seeing migrations as a disturbance of basic contact with familiar surroundings (a disruption of routines that might enable aspects of practical knowledge to be brought to discursive consciousness). In other words, the project approached transnational migration as an opportunity to explore senses of place (and the dwelling-journey relationship, see Seamon, 1989). On the one hand, then, the research participants were able to talk about aspects of the lifeworlds they had known, practically and emotionally, prior to their migrations, while on the other hand it was possible to understand something of how these young people were re-establishing familiarity in initially strange physical surroundings. Interestingly, the project's empirical data contained a considerable amount of material on diverse forms of mobility (Urry, 2000). These diverse mobilities included the everyday movements (Seamon, 1979) of walking, driving and travelling by bus or train, but they also included the long-distance mobilities of objects and the participants' technologically mediated mobilities via trans-European transport and communication links. Indeed, those transport and communication links, along with the inhabiting of certain media environments, contributed significantly to the historical and cultural specificity of the migrants' experiences (to their experiences of reach, see Buttimer, 1980; Silverstone, 1994).

One way of thinking about the project I have just summarised is as an example of non-media-centric media studies. In the collaborative research that Monika Metykova and I were involved in, electronic media were clearly of interest, given their affordances for instantaneous communications and intimacy at a distance, yet our commitment was to an investigation of the media uses of trans-European migrants in the context of other social practices and processes. Such an approach is valuable, I believe, because it can highlight the connections between, say, mobile-phone and internet use, international air travel and practices of walking and driving in the city. These connections, and their overall importance for understanding skilful bodily orientation and habitation (that is, getting around and feeling comfortable in various environments), would be likely to be missed by a more media-centred view.

More generally, I want to suggest that this book as a whole, like much of my earlier theoretical and empirical work, provides an illustration of what Morley (2007, 2009) names a non-media-centric form of media studies. How, though, can media studies possibly be 'non-media-centric'? Surely those who are working in the field of media studies will necessarily 'centre' media in their investigations and explanations of social life?

Broadly in line with Morley (2007, p. 1), I am arguing that media research requires an analytical framework that pays 'sufficient attention to the particularities of ... media ... without reifying their status and thus isolating them from the dynamics of the ... contexts in which they operate'. As I put it at one point in my last book:

> A common misconception ... is ... that media studies are simply about 'studying media'. ... They are not, or, at least, I want to argue very strongly that they should not be. ... Instead, it is necessary to appreciate the complex ways in which media of communication are bound up with wider institutional, technological and political processes in the modern world.
>
> (Moores, 2005, p. 3)

I therefore stand alongside Morley (2007, p. 200) when he asserts that 'we need to "decentre" ... media ... in our analytical framework'. In part, he continues, this is 'so as to ... understand the ways in which media processes and everyday life are interwoven with each other' (ibid.). The implication of his second statement here is that everyday living is one of the things that need to be centred in non-media-centric media studies, and this centring of the everyday has been an evolving concern of mine ever since I wrote an undergraduate dissertation, back in 1985, on the ways in which radio had gradually become 'interwoven' with household practices during the 1920s and 1930s (see Moores, 2009 [1988]). It has been an evolving concern of Morley's, too, which in his case can be traced back to the qualitative empirical research that he was doing at the same time on television's interweaving with domestic routines and relationships (Morley, 1986). To restate, an appreciation of media's distinctive features (what Morley, 2007, p. 1, calls their 'particularities') is crucial, because they differ from other material objects in everyday living such as foodstuffs or furnishings, as well as from each other, and yet it is precisely the relationship between media uses and a range of accompanying practices that has to be investigated.

Looking back at my own work over many years on issues of media in 'everyday life' (see especially Moores, 1993a, 1996, 2000), I now realise that a key difficulty for me was in finding a conceptual vocabulary that could do justice to the lived experiences of the everyday. When I was a student, and for a long time after, the field of media studies was strongly influenced by 'structuralist' and 'post-structuralist' theoretical perspectives. Most notably, a Marxist-inflected semiotic approach involved conceptualising 'media processes' primarily in terms of ideology, representation, codes, sign-systems, texts and readings. It is true that the field's development was shaped, in addition, by a 'culturalist' tradition (also largely Marxist-inflected), which allowed considerably more room for an exploration of the experiential dimension of contemporary living, but even this tradition of work could not illuminate, at least to my satisfaction, what I now think of as people's everyday environmental experiences, including their practical, embodied and sensuous involvements with media of communication. Only in recent years, since engaging with phenomenological philosophy and phenomenologically inspired approaches in the social sciences and humanities, have I felt that I am finding an adequate set of concepts for 'my' non-media-centric media studies. Of course, as I have shown, phenomenological analysis has its limitations. However, these are, in my view, far outweighed by its numerous positive contributions to the investigation of quotidian cultures.

Interestingly, Morley (2009, p. 114), who was one of the pioneers of critical social-semiotic research on the encoding and decoding of media texts in the 1970s, justifies his call for 'materialist' non-media-centric media studies by referring (and returning) to Marxism, writing that: 'Marx and Engels defined communication broadly enough to include not only ... the instruments for transmitting information but also the material transportation infrastructures of their day.' He observes with regret that, within media studies, attention to 'the movement of information' has tended to be 'to the neglect of the analysis of the corresponding movements of objects ... and persons' (ibid.), and he goes on to identify, as I have done, the relevance of Urry's social theory of mobilities for non-media-centric media studies today. It is evident that Morley is less inclined than I am to turn to phenomenological perspectives. Still, on the matter of his reference to Marxism, it is worth noting that contemporary philosopher Don Ihde (1990, p. 27) sees phenomenology as belonging to the same 'family of praxis philosophies' as Marx's original historical materialism.

Where Morley (2009, p. 115) and I are completely in agreement is in suggesting that many of those who are currently working in the field of media studies ought to be taking its 'interdisciplinary roots more seriously'. When the 'critical paradigm' of modern media studies was being developed in Britain by Morley and others in the 1970s, and indeed when I was an undergraduate, from the early to mid-1980s, on the UK's first degree programme in media studies, the field was markedly interdisciplinary. My lecturers came from a variety of disciplinary backgrounds in the social sciences and humanities, and, along with my fellow students, I was encouraged to read widely across the boundaries of academic disciplines. The abiding memory that I have of that time is one of trying to get to grips with a challenging but exciting mix of ideas. Although the reading that I do these days is very different (for example, I no longer spend hours on end immersed in debates about the politics of 'classic realist' or avant-garde film texts!), I hope not to have lost the sense of interdisciplinary adventure that was instilled in me back then. Above all, it is that spirit of adventure that I would like to pass on to the readers of this book.

These days, the field of media studies looks more like an academic discipline in its own right. It remains young enough to suffer attacks from outsiders, who, in my view, mistakenly question its intellectual value and even the purpose of its existence. However, it now has a firm foothold in universities across the world, with an array of degree programmes and its own departments, national and international subject associations, and so on. This emerging disciplinary status has clear advantages, and those who were involved in the field at an early stage could surely not have imagined the remarkable scale of its growth over the past four decades. Yet the increasingly established character of media studies brings some disadvantages too. One major drawback, for me, is that the field feels more insular than it did in its formative years. It is my contention that media studies are at their strongest when they are open to ideas that are circulating elsewhere in the social sciences and humanities, and in this book I have pointed in particular to perspectives from geography, philosophy, anthropology and sociology, encouraging readers to go well beyond what would normally be regarded as the field's boundaries. Equally, though, I am proposing that many of those who are working in such disciplines do not pay enough attention to media and their uses. Having provided an interdisciplinary account of the relations between media, place and mobility, it is my hope that the book will be helpful not only in media studies but also, more broadly, to anyone who is concerned to understand the dynamics of dwelling and travelling in contemporary society.

Bibliography

Adams, P. C. (1992) 'Television as Gathering Place', *Annals of the Association of American Geographers* vol. 82, pp. 117–35.

Adams, P. C. (2009) *Geographies of Media and Communication* (Malden, MA: Wiley-Blackwell).

Adey, P. (2010) *Mobility* (London: Routledge).

Aksoy, A. and K. Robins (2003) 'Banal Transnationalism: The Difference That Television Makes', in K. Karim (ed.) *The Media of Diaspora* (London: Routledge).

Amin, A. and N. Thrift (2002) *Cities: Reimagining the Urban* (Cambridge: Polity).

Anderson, B. (2008) '*For Space* (2005): Doreen Massey', in P. Hubbard, R. Kitchin and G. Valentine (eds) *Key Texts in Human Geography* (London: Sage).

Anderson, B. (2009) 'Non-representational Theory', in D. Gregory, R. Johnston, G. Pratt, M. J. Watts and S. Whatmore (eds) *The Dictionary of Human Geography* (Malden, MA: Wiley-Blackwell).

Anderson, B. and P. Harrison (eds) (2010a) *Taking-place: Non-representational Theories and Geography* (Farnham: Ashgate).

Anderson, B. and P. Harrison (2010b) 'The Promise of Non-representational Theories', in B. Anderson and P. Harrison (eds) *Taking-place: Non-representational Theories and Geography* (Farnham: Ashgate).

Aneesh, A. (2006) *Virtual Migration: The Programming of Globalization* (Durham, NC: Duke University Press).

Ang, I. (1996 [1990]) 'Melodramatic Identifications: Television Fiction and Women's Fantasy', in *Living Room Wars: Rethinking Media Audiences for a Postmodern World* (London: Routledge).

Appadurai, A. (1986) 'Introduction: Commodities and the Politics of Value', in A. Appadurai (ed.) *The Social Life of Things: Commodities in Cultural Perspective* (Cambridge: Cambridge University Press).

Appadurai, A. (1996) *Modernity at Large: Cultural Dimensions of Globalization* (Minneapolis: University of Minnesota Press).

Augé, M. (2009 [1995]) *Non-places* (London: Verso).

Bachelard, G. (1969) *The Poetics of Space* (Boston, MA: Beacon).

Bailey, O., M. Georgiou and R. Harindranath (eds) (2007) *Transnational Lives and the Media: Re-imagining Diaspora* (Basingstoke: Palgrave Macmillan).

Bakardjieva, M. (2005) *Internet Society: The Internet in Everyday Life* (London: Sage).

Bassett, C. (2003) 'How Many Movements?', in M. Bull and L. Back (eds) *The Auditory Culture Reader* (Oxford: Berg).

Bauman, Z. (1998) *Globalization: The Human Consequences* (Cambridge: Polity).

Bausinger, H. (1984) 'Media, Technology and Daily Life', *Media, Culture and Society* vol. 6, pp. 343–51.

Bell, D. (2007) *Cyberculture Theorists: Manuel Castells and Donna Haraway* (London: Routledge).

Bennett, T. (2005) 'The Media Sensorium: Cultural Technologies, the Senses and Society', in M. Gillespie (ed.) *Media Audiences* (Maidenhead: Open University Press).

Berger, P. L. and T. Luckmann (1991 [1966]) *The Social Construction of Reality: A Treatise in the Sociology of Knowledge* (London: Penguin).

Berker, T., M. Hartmann, Y. Punie and K. J. Ward (eds) (2006) *Domestication of Media and Technology* (Maidenhead: Open University Press).

Bird, J., B. Curtis, T. Putnam, G. Robertson and L. Tickner (eds) (1993) *Mapping the Futures: Local Cultures, Global Change* (London: Routledge).

Blattner, W. (2006) *Heidegger's Being and Time: A Reader's Guide* (London: Continuum).

Blumler, J. G. and E. Katz (eds) (1974) *The Uses of Mass Communications: Current Perspectives on Gratifications Research* (Beverly Hills, CA: Sage).

Boden, D. and H. L. Molotch (1994) 'The Compulsion of Proximity', in R. Friedland and D. Boden (eds) *NowHere: Space, Time and Modernity* (Berkeley: University of California Press).

Bourdieu, P. (1977) *Outline of a Theory of Practice* (Cambridge: Cambridge University Press).

Bourdieu, P. (1984) *Distinction: A Social Critique of the Judgement of Taste* (London: Routledge and Kegan Paul).

Bourdieu, P. (1990) *The Logic of Practice* (Cambridge: Polity).

Bourdieu, P. (2000) *Pascalian Meditations* (Cambridge: Polity).

Bourdieu, P. and L. J. D. Wacquant (1992) *An Invitation to Reflexive Sociology* (Cambridge: Polity).

Brown, A. (1998) 'Up Close from a Distance: Media and the Culture of Cricket', in R. Dickinson, R. Harindranath and O. Linné (eds) *Approaches to Audiences: A Reader* (London: Arnold).

Bull, M. (2000) *Sounding Out the City: Personal Stereos and the Management of Everyday Life* (Oxford: Berg).

Bull, M. (2001) 'Soundscapes of the Car: A Critical Study of Automobile Habitation', in D. Miller (ed.) *Car Cultures* (Oxford: Berg).

Bull, M. (2007) *Sound Moves: iPod Culture and Urban Experience* (London: Routledge).

Büscher, M., J. Urry and K. Witchger (eds) (2011) *Mobile Methods* (London: Routledge).

Buttimer, A. (1976) 'Grasping the Dynamism of Lifeworld', *Annals of the Association of American Geographers* vol. 66, pp. 277–92.

Buttimer, A. (1980) 'Home, Reach and the Sense of Place', in A. Buttimer and D. Seamon (eds) *The Human Experience of Space and Place* (London: Croom Helm).

Buttimer, A. and D. Seamon (eds) (1980) *The Human Experience of Space and Place* (London: Croom Helm).

Cameron, D. (2000) *Good to Talk? Living and Working in a Communication Culture* (London: Sage).

Carman, T. (2008) *Merleau-Ponty* (London: Routledge).

Casey, E. S. (2002) 'Body, Self, and Landscape: A Geophilosophical Inquiry into the Place-world', in P. C. Adams, S. Hoelscher and K. E. Till (eds) *Textures of Place: Exploring Humanist Geographies* (Minneapolis: University of Minnesota Press).

Castells, M. (1996) *The Rise of the Network Society* (Malden, MA: Blackwell).

Castells, M. (2000) 'Grassrooting the Space of Flows', in J. O. Wheeler, Y. Aoyama and B. Warf (eds) *Cities in the Telecommunications Age: The Fracturing of Geographies* (New York: Routledge).

Castells, M. (2001) *The Internet Galaxy: Reflections on the Internet, Business and Society* (Oxford: Oxford University Press).

Castells, M. (2005) 'Space of Flows, Space of Places: Materials for a Theory of Urbanism in the Information Age', in B. Sanyal (ed.) *Comparative Planning Cultures* (New York: Routledge).

Castells, M., M. Fernández-Ardèvol, J. L. Qiu and A. Sey (2007) *Mobile Communication and Society: A Global Perspective* (Cambridge, MA: MIT Press).

Charlesworth, S. J. (2000) *A Phenomenology of Working Class Experience* (Cambridge: Cambridge University Press).

Clifford, J. (1992) 'Traveling Cultures', in L. Grossberg, C. Nelson and P. A. Treichler (eds) *Cultural Studies* (New York: Routledge).

Clifford, J. (1997) *Routes: Travel and Translation in the Late Twentieth Century* (Cambridge, MA: Harvard University Press).

Couldry, N. (2001) 'Everyday Royal Celebrity', in D. Morley and K. Robins (eds) *British Cultural Studies: Geography, Nationality and Identity* (Oxford: Oxford University Press).

Couldry, N. (2006) *Listening beyond the Echoes: Media, Ethics, and Agency in an Uncertain World* (Boulder, CO: Paradigm).

Couldry, N. (2010) 'Theorising Media as Practice', in B. Bräuchler and J. Postill (eds) *Theorising Media and Practice* (Oxford: Berghahn).

Couldry, N., A. Hepp and F. Krotz (eds) (2010) *Media Events in a Global Age* (London: Routledge).

Cresswell, T. (2002) 'Introduction: Theorizing Place', in G. Verstraete and T. Cresswell (eds) *Mobilizing Place, Placing Mobility: The Politics of Representation in a Globalized World* (Amsterdam: Rodopi).

Cresswell, T. (2004) *Place: A Short Introduction* (Malden, MA: Blackwell).

Cresswell, T. (2006) *On the Move: Mobility in the Modern Western World* (New York: Routledge).

Cresswell, T. (2008) '*Space and Place* (1977): Yi-Fu Tuan', in P. Hubbard, R. Kitchin and G. Valentine (eds) *Key Texts in Human Geography* (London: Sage).

Cresswell, T. and P. Merriman (eds) (2011) *Geographies of Mobilities: Practices, Spaces, Subjects* (Farnham: Ashgate).

Crossley, N. (2001) *The Social Body: Habit, Identity and Desire* (London: Sage).

Cwerner, S., S. Kesselring and J. Urry (eds) (2009) *Aeromobilities* (London: Routledge).

Dayan, D. (1999) 'Media and Diasporas', in J. Gripsrud (ed.) *Television and Common Knowledge* (London: Routledge).

Dayan, D. and E. Katz (1992) *Media Events: The Live Broadcasting of History* (Cambridge, MA: Harvard University Press).

de Certeau, M. (1984) *The Practice of Everyday Life* (Berkeley: University of California Press).

de Certeau, M. (1985) 'Practices of Space', in M. Blonsky (ed.) *On Signs* (Baltimore, MD: Johns Hopkins University Press).

Dewsbury, J.-D., J. Wylie, P. Harrison and M. Rose (2002) 'Enacting Geographies', *Geoforum* vol. 32, pp. 437–41.

Dreyfus, H. L. (1991) *Being-in-the-world: A Commentary on Heidegger's* Being and Time, Division I (Cambridge, MA: MIT Press).

Dreyfus, H. L. (2001) *On the Internet* (London: Routledge).

Duruz, J. and C. Johnson (1999) 'Mourning at a Distance: Australians and the Death of a British Princess', in A. Kear and D. L. Steinberg (eds) *Mourning Diana: Nation, Culture and the Performance of Grief* (London: Routledge).

Edensor, T. (2002) *National Identity, Popular Culture and Everyday Life* (Oxford: Berg).

Elliott, A. and J. Urry (2010) *Mobile Lives* (London: Routledge).

Fincham, B., M. McGuinness and L. Murray (eds) (2010) *Mobile Methodologies* (Basingstoke: Palgrave Macmillan).

Fiske, J. (1989) *Understanding Popular Culture* (Boston, MA: Unwin Hyman).

Garfinkel, H. (1984 [1967]) *Studies in Ethnomethodology* (Cambridge: Polity).

Gauntlett, D. and A. Hill (1999) *TV Living: Television, Culture and Everyday Life* (London: Routledge).

Geertz, C. (1973) *The Interpretation of Cultures: Selected Essays* (New York: Basic Books).

Gibson, J. J. (1986 [1979]) *The Ecological Approach to Visual Perception* (Hillsdale, NJ: Lawrence Erlbaum).

Giddens, A. (1984) *The Constitution of Society: Outline of the Theory of Structuration* (Cambridge: Polity).

Giddens, A. (1990) *The Consequences of Modernity* (Cambridge: Polity).

Giddens, A. (1991) *Modernity and Self-identity: Self and Society in the Late Modern Age* (Cambridge: Polity).

Gillespie, M. (1995) *Television, Ethnicity and Cultural Change* (London: Routledge).

Gillespie, M. (2000) 'Transnational Communications and Diaspora Communities', in S. Cottle (ed.) *Ethnic Minorities and the Media: Changing Cultural Boundaries* (Buckingham: Open University Press).

Gillespie, M. (2002) 'Dynamics of Diasporas: South Asian Media and Transnational Cultural Politics', in G. Stald and T. Tufte (eds) *Global Encounters: Media and Cultural Transformation* (Luton: University of Luton Press).

Goffman, E. (1981) 'Radio Talk', in *Forms of Talk* (Philadelphia: University of Pennsylvania Press).

Goffman, E. (1990 [1959]) *The Presentation of Self in Everyday Life* (London: Penguin).

Goggin, G. (2006) *Cell Phone Culture: Mobile Technology in Everyday Life* (London: Routledge).

Goggin, G. (ed.) (2008) *Mobile Phone Cultures* (London: Routledge).

Gray, A. (1987) 'Behind Closed Doors: Video Recorders in the Home', in H. Baehr and G. Dyer (eds) *Boxed In: Women and Television* (London: Pandora).

Gray, A. (1992) *Video Playtime: The Gendering of a Leisure Technology* (London: Routledge).

Gray, J. (2003 [1999]) 'Open Spaces and Dwelling Places: Being at Home on Hill Farms in the Scottish Borders', in S. M. Low and D. Lawrence-Zúñinga (eds) *The Anthropology of Space and Place: Locating Culture* (Malden, MA: Blackwell).

Green, N. and L. Haddon (2009) *Mobile Communications: An Introduction to New Media* (Oxford: Berg).

Grosz, E. (1994) *Volatile Bodies: Toward a Corporeal Feminism* (Bloomington: Indiana University Press).

Gumpert, G. and R. Cathcart (eds) (1979) *Inter/Media: Interpersonal Communication in a Media World* (New York: Oxford University Press).

Hall, S. (1980) 'Encoding/Decoding', in S. Hall, D. Hobson, A. Lowe and P. Willis (eds) *Culture, Media, Language: Working Papers in Cultural Studies, 1972–79* (London: Hutchinson).

Hall, S. (1992) 'The Question of Cultural Identity', in S. Hall, D. Held and T. McGrew (eds) *Modernity and Its Futures* (Cambridge: Polity).

Hannam, K., M. Sheller and J. Urry (2006) 'Editorial: Mobilities, Immobilities and Moorings', *Mobilities* vol. 1, pp. 1–22.

Hannerz, U. (1996) *Transnational Connections: Culture, People, Places* (London: Routledge).

Hannerz, U. (2001) 'Thinking about Culture in a Global Ecumene', in J. Lull (ed.) *Culture in the Communication Age* (London: Routledge).

Hansen, M. B. N. (2006) *Bodies in Code: Interfaces with Digital Media* (New York: Routledge).

Harvey, D. (1989) *The Condition of Postmodernity: An Enquiry into the Origins of Cultural Change* (Oxford: Blackwell).

Hass, L. (2008) *Merleau-Ponty's Philosophy* (Bloomington: Indiana University Press).

Hassan, R. (2004) *Media, Politics and the Network Society* (Maidenhead: Open University Press).

Haythornthwaite, C. and B. Wellman (2002) 'The Internet in Everyday Life: An Introduction', in B. Wellman and C. Haythornthwaite (eds) *The Internet in Everyday Life* (Malden, MA: Blackwell).

Heidegger, M. (1962) *Being and Time* (Oxford: Blackwell).

Heidegger, M. (1993 [1971]) 'Building Dwelling Thinking', in D. F. Krell (ed.) *Martin Heidegger: Basic Writings* (London: Routledge).

Horst, H. A. and D. Miller (2006) *The Cell Phone: An Anthropology of Communication* (Oxford: Berg).

Horton, D. and R. R. Wohl (1956) 'Mass Communication and Para-social Interaction: Observations on Intimacy at a Distance', *Psychiatry* vol. 19, pp. 215–29.

Howes, D. (2003) *Sensual Relations: Engaging the Senses in Culture and Social Theory* (Ann Arbor: University of Michigan Press).

Hutchby, I. (2001) *Conversation and Technology: From the Telephone to the Internet* (Cambridge: Polity).

Ihde, D. (1990) *Technology and the Lifeworld: From Garden to Earth* (Bloomington: Indiana University Press).

Ihde, D. (2002) *Bodies in Technology* (Minneapolis: University of Minnesota Press).

Ingold, T. (2000) *The Perception of the Environment: Essays in Livelihood, Dwelling and Skill* (London: Routledge).

Ingold, T. (2004) 'Culture on the Ground: The World Perceived through the Feet', *Journal of Material Culture* vol. 9, pp. 315–40.

Ingold, T. (2007) *Lines: A Brief History* (London: Routledge).

Ingold, T. (2008) 'Bindings against Boundaries: Entanglements of Life in an Open World', *Environment and Planning A* vol. 40, pp. 1796–810.

Innis, H. A. (1951) *The Bias of Communication* (Toronto, ON: University of Toronto Press).

Jackson, M. (ed.) (1996) *Things as They Are: New Directions in Phenomenological Anthropology* (Bloomington: Indiana University Press).

Jensen, J. F. (1999) '"Interactivity": Tracking a New Concept in Media and Communication Studies', in P. A. Mayer (ed.) *Computer Media and Communication: A Reader* (Oxford: Oxford University Press).

Karim, K. (ed.) (2003) *The Media of Diaspora* (London: Routledge).

Katz, J. (1999) *How Emotions Work* (Chicago, IL: University of Chicago Press).

Katz, J. E. (2006) *Magic in the Air: Mobile Communication and the Transformation of Social Life* (New Brunswick, NJ: Transaction).

Katz, J. E. and M. A. Aakhus (eds) (2002) *Perpetual Contact: Mobile Communication, Private Talk, Public Performance* (Cambridge: Cambridge University Press).

Kendall, L. (2002) *Hanging Out in the Virtual Pub: Masculinities and Relationships Online* (Berkeley: University of California Press).

King, R. and N. Wood (eds) (2001) *Media and Migration: Constructions of Mobility and Difference* (London: Routledge).

Lally, E. (2002) *At Home with Computers* (Oxford: Berg).

Larsen, J., J. Urry and K. Axhausen (2006) *Mobilities, Networks, Geographies* (Aldershot: Ashgate).

Larsen, P. (1999) 'Imaginary Spaces: Television, Technology and Everyday Consciousness', in J. Gripsrud (ed.) *Television and Common Knowledge* (London: Routledge).

Lee, J. and T. Ingold (2006) 'Fieldwork on Foot: Perceiving, Routing, Socializing', in S. Coleman and P. Collins (eds) *Locating the Field: Space, Place and Context in Anthropology* (Oxford: Berg).

Lefebvre, H. (1991) *The Production of Space* (Malden, MA: Blackwell).

Lefebvre, H. (2004) *Rhythmanalysis: Space, Time and Everyday Life* (London: Continuum).

Lemert, C. and A. Branaman (eds) (1997) *The Goffman Reader* (Malden, MA: Blackwell).

Leyshon, A. (1995) 'Annihilating Space? The Speed-up of Communications', in J. Allen and C. Hamnett (eds) *A Shrinking World? Global Unevenness and Inequality* (Oxford: Oxford University Press).

Ling, R. (2004) *The Mobile Connection: The Cell Phone's Impact on Society* (Amsterdam: Elsevier).

Ling, R. and J. Donner (2009) *Mobile Communication* (Cambridge: Polity).

Littau, K. (2006) *Theories of Reading: Books, Bodies and Bibliomania* (Cambridge: Polity).

McGuigan, J. (1999) *Modernity and Postmodern Culture* (Buckingham: Open University Press).

McLuhan, E. and F. Zingrone (eds) (1997) *Essential McLuhan* (London: Routledge).

McLuhan, M. (1994 [1964]) *Understanding Media: The Extensions of Man* (Cambridge, MA: MIT Press).

Massey, D. (1991) 'A Global Sense of Place', *Marxism Today*, June, pp. 24–9.

Massey, D. (1994) *Space, Place and Gender* (Cambridge: Polity).

Massey, D. (1995) 'The Conceptualization of Place', in D. Massey and P. Jess (eds) *A Place in the World? Places, Cultures and Globalization* (Oxford: Oxford University Press).

Massey, D. (2005) *For Space* (London: Sage).

Massey, D. (2007) *World City* (Cambridge: Polity).

Merleau-Ponty, M. (2002 [1962]) *Phenomenology of Perception* (London: Routledge).

Merleau-Ponty, M. (2004 [1964]) 'Merleau-Ponty's Prospectus of His Work', in T. Baldwin (ed.) *Maurice Merleau-Ponty: Basic Writings* (London: Routledge).

Meyrowitz, J. (1979) 'Television and Interpersonal Behavior: Codes of Perception and Response', in G. Gumpert and R. Cathcart (eds) *Inter/Media: Interpersonal Communication in a Media World* (New York: Oxford University Press).

Meyrowitz, J. (1985) *No Sense of Place: The Impact of Electronic Media on Social Behavior* (New York: Oxford University Press).

Meyrowitz, J. (1994) 'Medium Theory', in D. Crowley and D. Mitchell (eds) *Communication Theory Today* (Cambridge: Polity).

Meyrowitz, J. (2003) 'Canonic Anti-text: Marshall McLuhan's *Understanding Media*', in E. Katz, J. D. Peters, T. Liebes and A. Orloff (eds) *Canonic Texts in Media Research: Are There Any? Should There Be? How about These?* (Cambridge: Polity).

Meyrowitz, J. (2005) 'The Rise of Glocality: New Senses of Place and Identity in the Global Village', in K. Nyíri (ed.) *A Sense of Place: The Global and the Local in Mobile Communication* (Vienna: Passagen Verlag).

Miller, D. (2010) *Stuff* (Cambridge: Polity).

Miller, D. and D. Slater (2000) *The Internet: An Ethnographic Approach* (Oxford: Berg).

Mitchell, W. J. (1995) *City of Bits: Space, Place, and the Infobahn* (Cambridge, MA: MIT Press).

Moores, S. (1993a) *Interpreting Audiences: The Ethnography of Media Consumption* (London: Sage).

Moores, S. (1993b) 'Television, Geography and "Mobile Privatization"', *European Journal of Communication* vol. 8, pp. 365–79.

Moores, S. (1996) *Satellite Television and Everyday Life: Articulating Technology* (Luton: John Libbey Media).

Moores, S. (2000) *Media and Everyday Life in Modern Society* (Edinburgh: Edinburgh University Press).

Moores, S. (2004) 'The Doubling of Place: Electronic Media, Time-space Arrangements and Social Relationships', in N. Couldry and A. McCarthy (eds) *Media/Space: Place, Scale and Culture in a Media Age* (London: Routledge).

Moores, S. (2005) *Media/Theory: Thinking about Media and Communications* (London: Routledge).

Moores, S. (2006) 'Media Uses and Everyday Environmental Experiences: A Positive Critique of Phenomenological Geography', *Participations* vol. 3 no. 2, available at <http://www.participations.org>.

Moores, S. (2007) 'Media and Senses of Place: On Situational and Phenomenological Geographies', Media@LSE Electronic Working Paper 12, London School of Economics and Political Science, available at <http://www.lse.ac.uk/collections/media@lse>.

Moores, S. (2008) 'Conceptualizing Place in a World of Flows', in A. Hepp, F. Krotz, S. Moores and C. Winter (eds) *Connectivity, Networks and Flows: Conceptualizing Contemporary Communications* (Cresskill, NJ: Hampton).

Moores, S. (2009 [1988]) ' "The Box on the Dresser": Memories of Early Radio and Everyday Life', in A. Crisell (ed.) *Radio: Critical Concepts in Media and Cultural Studies, Vol. 3 – Audiences, Identities and Communities* (London: Routledge).

Moores, S. and M. Metykova (2009) 'Knowing How to Get Around: Place, Migration, and Communication', *Communication Review* vol. 12, pp. 313–26.

Moores, S. and M. Metykova (2010) ' "I Didn't Realize How Attached I Am": On the Environmental Experiences of Trans-European Migrants', *European Journal of Cultural Studies* vol. 13, pp. 171–89.

Morgan, D. (2009) *Acquaintances: The Space between Intimates and Strangers* (Maidenhead: Open University Press).

Morley, D. (1980) *The Nationwide Audience: Structure and Decoding* (London: BFI).

Morley, D. (1986) *Family Television: Cultural Power and Domestic Leisure* (London: Comedia).

Morley, D. (1992) *Television, Audiences and Cultural Studies* (London: Routledge).

Morley, D. (2000) *Home Territories: Media, Mobility and Identity* (London: Routledge).

Morley, D. (2003) 'What's "Home" Got to Do with It? Contradictory Dynamics in the Domestication of Technology and the Dislocation of Domesticity', *European Journal of Cultural Studies* vol. 6, pp. 435–58.

Morley, D. (2007) *Media, Modernity and Technology: The Geography of the New* (London: Routledge).

Morley, D. (2009) 'For a Materialist, Non-media-centric Media Studies', *Television and New Media* vol. 10, pp. 114–16.

Morley, D. (2010) 'Television as a Means of Transport: Digital Technologies and Transmodal Systems', in J. Gripsrud (ed.) *Relocating Television: Television in the Digital Context* (London: Routledge).

Morley, D. (forthcoming) *Communications* (Oxford: Wiley-Blackwell).

Nunes, M. (2006) *Cyberspaces of Everyday Life* (Minneapolis: University of Minnesota Press).

Nyíri, K. (ed.) (2005) *A Sense of Place: The Global and the Local in Mobile Communication* (Vienna: Passagen Verlag).

Olwig, K. F. and K. Hastrup (1997) 'Introduction', in K. F. Olwig and K. Hastrup (eds) *Siting Culture: The Shifting Anthropological Object* (London: Routledge).

O'Neill, M. (2007) 'Re-imagining Diaspora through Ethno-mimesis: Humiliation, Human Dignity and Belonging', in O. Bailey, M. Georgiou and R. Harindranath (eds) *Transnational Lives and the Media: Re-imagining Diaspora* (Basingstoke: Palgrave Macmillan).

Peterson, M. A. (2010) ' "But It Is My Habit to Read the *Times*": Metaculture and Practice in the Reading of Indian Newspapers', in B. Bräuchler and J. Postill (eds) *Theorising Media and Practice* (Oxford: Berghahn).

Pink, S. (2009) *Doing Sensory Ethnography* (London: Sage).

Pred, A. (1996 [1977]) 'The Choreography of Existence: Comments on Hägerstrand's Time-geography and Its Usefulness', in J. Agnew, D. N. Livingstone and A. Rogers (eds) *Human Geography: An Essential Anthology* (Malden, MA: Blackwell).

Relph, E. (2008 [1976]) *Place and Placelessness* (London: Pion).

Richardson, I. (2008) 'Pocket Technospaces: The Bodily Incorporation of Mobile Media', in G. Goggin (ed.) *Mobile Phone Cultures* (London: Routledge).

Roberts, B. (2006) *Micro Social Theory* (Basingstoke: Palgrave Macmillan).

Rodaway, P. (2004) 'Yi-Fu Tuan', in P. Hubbard, R. Kitchin and G. Valentine (eds) *Key Thinkers on Space and Place* (London: Sage).

Romdenh-Romluc, K. (2011) *Merleau-Ponty and* Phenomenology of Perception (London: Routledge).

Sacks, H. (1995) *Lectures on Conversation* (Oxford: Blackwell).

Scannell, P. (1995) 'For a Phenomenology of Radio and Television', *Journal of Communication* vol. 45 no. 3, pp. 4–19.

Scannell, P. (1996) *Radio, Television and Modern Life: A Phenomenological Approach* (Oxford: Blackwell).

Scannell, P. (2007) *Media and Communication* (London: Sage).

Scannell, P. (forthcoming) *Television and the Meaning of 'Live'* (Cambridge: Polity).

Scannell, P. and D. Cardiff (1991) *A Social History of British Broadcasting: 1922–1939, Serving the Nation* (Oxford: Blackwell).

Schegloff, E. A. (2002) 'Beginnings in the Telephone', in J. E. Katz and M. A. Aakhus (eds) *Perpetual Contact: Mobile Communication, Private Talk, Public Performance* (Cambridge: Cambridge University Press).

Schutz, A. (1967) *The Phenomenology of the Social World* (Evanston, IL: Northwestern University Press).

Seamon, D. (1979) *A Geography of the Lifeworld: Movement, Rest, and Encounter* (New York: St Martin's Press).

Seamon, D. (1980) 'Body-subject, Time-space Routines and Place-ballets', in A. Buttimer and D. Seamon (eds) *The Human Experience of Space and Place* (London: Croom Helm).

Seamon, D. (1989) 'Reconciling Old and New Worlds: The Dwelling–journey Relationship as Portrayed in Vilhelm Moberg's "Emigrant" Novels', in D. Seamon and R. Mugerauer (eds) *Dwelling, Place, and Environment: Towards a Phenomenology of Person and World* (New York: Columbia University Press).

Seamon, D. (2006) 'A Geography of the Lifeworld in Retrospect: A Response to Shaun Moores', *Participations* vol. 3 no. 2, available at <http://www.participations.org>.

Seamon, D. and J. Sowers (2008) 'Place and Placelessness (1976): Edward Relph', in P. Hubbard, R. Kitchin and G. Valentine (eds) *Key Texts in Human Geography* (London: Sage).

Sheller, M. (2008 [2004]) 'Automotive Emotions: Feeling the Car', in M. Greco and P. Stenner (eds) *Emotions: A Social Science Reader* (London: Routledge).

Sheller, M. and J. Urry (2006) 'The New Mobilities Paradigm', *Environment and Planning A* vol. 38, pp. 207–26.

Sibley, D. (1995) *Geographies of Exclusion: Society and Difference in the West* (London: Routledge).

Silverstone, R. (1989) 'Let Us Then Return to the Murmuring of Everyday Practices: A Note on Michel de Certeau, Television and Everyday Life', *Theory, Culture and Society* vol. 6, pp. 77–94.

Silverstone, R. (1990) 'Television and Everyday Life: Towards an Anthropology of the Television Audience', in M. Ferguson (ed.) *Public Communication: The New Imperatives – Future Directions for Media Research* (London: Sage).

Silverstone, R. (1991) 'From Audiences to Consumers: The Household and the Consumption of Information and Communication Technologies', *European Journal of Communication* vol. 6, pp. 135–54.

Silverstone, R. (1994) *Television and Everyday Life* (London: Routledge).

Silverstone, R. and L. Haddon (1996) 'Design and the Domestication of Information and Communication Technologies: Technical Change and Everyday Life', in R. Mansell and R. Silverstone (eds) *Communication by Design: The Politics of Communication Technologies* (Oxford: Oxford University Press).

Silverstone, R., E. Hirsch and D. Morley (1992) 'Information and Communication Technologies and the Moral Economy of the Household', in R. Silverstone and E. Hirsch (eds) *Consuming Technologies: Media and Information in Domestic Spaces* (London: Routledge).

Sudnow, D. (1993 [1979]) *Ways of the Hand: The Organization of Improvised Conduct* (Cambridge, MA: MIT Press).

Taylor, C. (2005) 'Merleau-Ponty and the Epistemological Picture', in T. Carman and M. Hansen (eds) *The Cambridge Companion to Merleau-Ponty* (New York: Cambridge University Press).

Taylor, C. (2006) 'Engaged Agency and Background in Heidegger', in C. B. Guignon (ed.) *The Cambridge Companion to Heidegger* (New York: Cambridge University Press).

Thompson, J. B. (1995) *The Media and Modernity: A Social Theory of the Media* (Cambridge: Polity).

Thompson, J. B. (2000) *Political Scandal: Power and Visibility in the Media Age* (Cambridge: Polity).

Thrift, N. (1996) *Spatial Formations* (London: Sage).

Thrift, N. (1999) 'Steps to an Ecology of Place', in D. Massey, J. Allen and P. Sarre (eds) *Human Geography Today* (Cambridge: Polity).

Thrift, N. (2004a) 'Driving in the City', *Theory, Culture and Society* vol. 21 nos 4/5, pp. 41–59.

Thrift, N. (2004b) 'Summoning Life', in P. Cloke, P. Crang and M. Goodwin (eds) *Envisioning Human Geographies* (London: Arnold).

Thrift, N. (2007) *Non-representational Theory: Space/Politics/Affect* (London: Routledge).

Thrift, N. (2009) 'Space: The Fundamental Stuff of Geography', in N. J. Clifford, S. L. Holloway, S. P. Rice and G. Valentine (eds) *Key Concepts in Geography* (London: Sage).

Tomlinson, J. (1999) *Globalization and Culture* (Cambridge: Polity).

Tomlinson, J. (2007) *The Culture of Speed: The Coming of Immediacy* (London: Sage).

Tuan, Y.-F. (1977) *Space and Place: The Perspective of Experience* (Minneapolis: University of Minnesota Press).

Tuan, Y.-F. (1996a [1974]) 'Space and Place: Humanistic Perspective', in J. Agnew, D. N. Livingstone and A. Rogers (eds) *Human Geography: An Essential Anthology* (Malden, MA: Blackwell).

Tuan, Y.-F. (1996b) *Cosmos and Hearth: A Cosmopolite's Viewpoint* (Minneapolis: University of Minnesota Press).

Tuan, Y.-F. (2004) 'Sense of Place: Its Relationship to Self and Time', in T. Mels (ed.) *Reanimating Places: A Geography of Rhythms* (Aldershot: Ashgate).

Turkle, S. (1996a) *Life on the Screen: Identity in the Age of the Internet* (London: Weidenfeld and Nicolson).

Turkle, S. (1996b) 'Parallel Lives: Working on Identity in Virtual Space', in D. Grodin and T. R. Lindlof (eds) *Constructing the Self in a Mediated World* (Thousand Oaks, CA: Sage).

Turnock, R. (2000) *Interpreting Diana: Television Audiences and the Death of a Princess* (London: BFI).

Urry, J. (1990) *The Tourist Gaze: Leisure and Travel in Contemporary Societies* (London: Sage).

Urry, J. (1995) *Consuming Places* (London: Routledge).

Urry, J. (2000) *Sociology beyond Societies: Mobilities for the Twenty-first Century* (London: Routledge).

Urry, J. (2002) 'Mobility and Proximity', *Sociology* vol. 36, pp. 255–74.

Urry, J. (2007) *Mobilities* (Cambridge: Polity).

van Dijk, J. A. G. M. (2006) *The Network Society: Social Aspects of New Media* (London: Sage).

Webster, F. (2002) *Theories of the Information Society* (London: Routledge).

Wellman, B. and C. Haythornthwaite (eds) (2002) *The Internet in Everyday Life* (Malden, MA: Blackwell).

Williams, R. (1990 [1974]) *Television: Technology and Cultural Form* (London: Routledge).

Willis, P. (2000) *The Ethnographic Imagination* (Cambridge: Polity).

Wittel, A. (2008) 'Towards a Network Sociality', in A. Hepp, F. Krotz, S. Moores and C. Winter (eds) *Connectivity, Networks and Flows: Conceptualizing Contemporary Communications* (Cresskill, NJ: Hampton).

Wood, H. (2007) 'The Mediated Conversational Floor: An Interactive Approach to Audience Reception Analysis', *Media, Culture and Society* vol. 29, pp. 75–103.

Wood, H. (2009) *Talking with Television: Women, Talk Shows, and Modern Self-reflexivity* (Urbana: University of Illinois Press).

Wylie, J. (2007) *Landscape* (London: Routledge).

Young, I. M. (2005 [1980]) 'Throwing Like a Girl: A Phenomenology of Feminine Body Comportment, Motility, and Spatiality', in *On Female Body Experience: 'Throwing Like a Girl' and Other Essays* (New York: Oxford University Press).

Index